Universal Fly Tying Guide

Dick Stewart

cover: SILVER DOCTOR

distributed by
THE STEPHEN GREENE PRESS
Fessenden Road, Brattleboro, Vermont 05301
And
UNIVERSAL VISE CORPORATION
16 Union Avenue, Westfield, Massachusetts 01085

Contents

ISBN 0-936644-00-1

Introduction

Any angler who learns to tie their own flies will discover that the new dimension of knowledge gained will carry forth to improve their streamside results. It is hoped that this book might serve to assist both beginning and more advanced tyers who are interested in acquiring such knowledge.

Recent years have added significantly to the availability of information regarding entomology as it relates to fishing. While many trout are still caught with flies and methods developed long ago, we are finding that more sophisticated flies and techniques are often required today. Frequently, local tackle shops are unable to supply adequate flies and this might germinate a desire to tie your own.

While the motivation to start fly tying may stem from different factors, many find it develops into a full hobby unto itself. Perhaps its appeal is in the opportunity to keep the hands and imagination busy on cold winter evening.

For beginners, the following advice cannot be overemphasized:

TAKE LESSONS — whether individual or through locally offered courses, competent instruction is far more worthwhile than trial and error methods.

USE GOOD MATERIALS — tyers often like to compare their flies against professionally tied samples and may find the results disappointing. Frequently the principal difference is in the materials used. No amount of skill can compensate for poor materials.

PRACTICE — to develop skills and gain familiarity with materials. Each feather or fur has different characteristics which can only be learned through continued handling.

CONSTRUCTION — here are some tips. DURABILITY — achieved primarily by keeping good tension on the thread throughout the tying procedure. The application of cements, while useful, is no substitute for proper tension. SPARSENESS — a common error is the excess use of material, thus overdressing the fly. Generally it's better to use too little than too much. SIZES — size is the most important factor in a fly. Having fewer patterns in a wide range of recommended sizes is better than to have many patterns all tied on size 12 hooks. PATTERNS — a variety of relatively easy, yet effective flies which a beginner might start with are:

Adams	Brown Bivisible	Hares Ear Nymph	Montana
Black Ant	Grey Hackle	Letort Hopper	Wooly Worm
Black Nose Dace	Hairwing Caddis	Mickey Finn	Zug Bug

As we develop our fly fishing skills the reward of catching fish on home tied flies begins to provide its own satisfaction beyond that of success measured by the quantity of fish killed. This often leads to the pleasure of problem solving within nature's realm and a wholistic appreciation of our environment. Your respectfulness toward our woods, water, and wildlife will be greatly appreciated by your fellow anglers.

Basic Tools

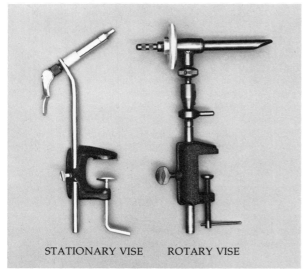

STATIONARY VISE   ROTARY VISE

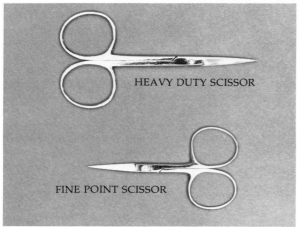

HEAVY DUTY SCISSOR

FINE POINT SCISSOR

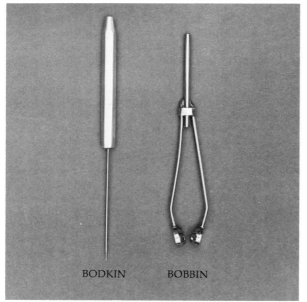

BODKIN   BOBBIN

HACKLE PLIER

4

VISE — The most important, and probably most expensive tool used in fly tying is the vise. Its primary function is to hold the hook securely. The basic type is called a stationary vise because it generally remains in one position, although it might have several possible adjustments. A second type, called the Rotary Vise, serves a dual function since it can be used as a stationary model but is also designed to rotate the hook to assist in the winding of materials. Many models are available at a wide range of prices, however, the least expensive models will usually prove inadequate. Features to look for include the ability to hold a wide range of hook sizes (especially the smaller hooks), smoothness of the finish, height adjustments, ease of operation, and the method of securing it to a desk or table.

SCISSORS — Small very sharp scissors with narrow fine points are indispensable for the detailed work of fly tying. Large finger holes are preferred by experienced tyers who keep the scissors on their fingers throughout the tying procedure. Heavier scissors are used on coarse materials primarily to protect the fine points and sharpness of the better pair. Most fly tying material suppliers offer scissors specially designed for this purpose. In some cases where the tips are too thick, the points can be carefully filed down from the outside. Both straight and curved blades are available with the choice being primarily a matter of personal preference.

BOBBIN — This is a tool which holds the spool of thread during the tying operation. The bobbin permits very accurate control over both the placement of each individual thread winding on the hook, and the very important thread tension which is the basis of building a strong, durable fly. Also the bobbin provides sufficient weight to prevent unravelling of thread when the hands must be free for other purposes.

BODKIN — A simple, inexpensive device consisting of a needle inserted into a handle for the sake of convenience. It is used for a great many operations such as applying head cement, picking out stray fibers, cleaning out the eye of a hook, separating fibers, and picking out dubbing fur. Some bodkins have a magnet built within to pick up hooks, others incorporate a half hitch tool as the handle.

HACKLE PLIERS — These are used to grip hackle feathers by the tips and to hold them securely as they are wound around or applied to the fly. They must have a firm grip as hackles are often very small and will slip out of the jaws quite easily. Sharp edges on the pliers will cut the feather and should be avoided. Low quality hackle pliers can be most exasperating.

Many tools have been designed to assist fly tyers with specific procedures. Some of the most useful include: **HALF HITCH TOOL** used to make half hitch knots at head, particularly useful on Muddler Minnow heads; **BOBBIN THREADER,** very inexpensive but saves on patience when trying to get thread through the bobbin tube, especially once it becomes clogged with wax; **TWEEZERS,** are very useful for picking up small hooks and for other occasions when you need to pick out very small feathers or fibers; **WHIP FINISHER,** a tool that requires practice to use properly, but once mastered, enables one to rapidly tie a whip finish knot, the most secure manner to tie off your thread upon completion of a fly; **HAIR STACKER,** is essentially a tube into which bucktail or other hair is inserted, tips downward, then tapped against desk or table, to evenly align the hair tips when used for wings or tails.

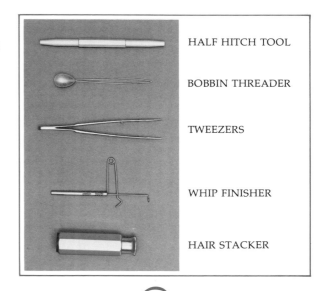

HALF HITCH TOOL

BOBBIN THREADER

TWEEZERS

WHIP FINISHER

HAIR STACKER

A hook is the most basic ingredient of a fly and has recently been appropriately described as the "backbone" of any fly. A wide variety of hooks are manufactured specifically for tying flies, with the majority being produced by O. Mustad & Sons in Norway. Various sizes of fly tying hooks are offered ranging from a designation of #1 to #28, with the highest number representing the smallest hook. Additionally, even larger hooks have size designations from #1/0 to #6/0 with higher numbers being larger hooks. The most commonly used sizes range from #6 to #16, although there is good occasion to use either larger or smaller hooks, particularly the latter. A second designation is hook length as shown in the accompanying chart which pictures hooks of the same size but of varying lengths. A stubby beetle imitation cannot be properly tied on a very long hook, and, conversely, a long slim minnow imitation requires the use of a longer shank. Hook wire weight is another consideration since a heavy wire is stronger and also helps a fly to sink. Light wire helps reduce the tendency to sink, is generally preferred for floating flies, and its smaller diameter offers less resistance to hook penetration. The most common hook eye type is turned down using tapered wire. A straight eye or turned up eye may be used to maximize the point clearance on very small flies, and these eye types are also used to achieve special effects on some flies. The most basic hook shapes are illustrated with there being little consensus as to which is best. Fly tying hooks generally have a straight bend, i.e. they are not offset to one side. Hooks can be converted to barbless or semi-barbed by carefully crimping down the barb with flat nose pliers. This seems to help hook penetration with no loss of holding ability. Another worthwhile practice is to sharpen all hooks before beginning to tie. Other styles such as keel, flybody, swedish, nymph form, parachute, and popper hooks are also available and worthy of attention and experimentation.

5

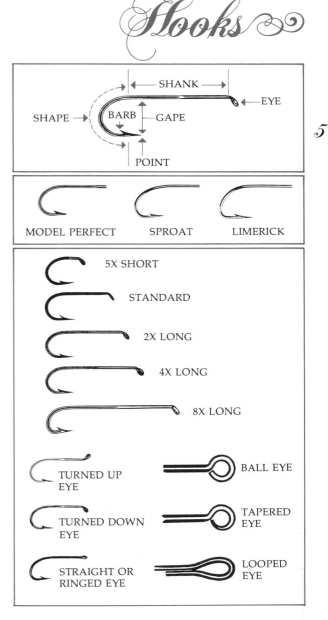

SHANK

EYE

SHAPE

BARB — GAPE

POINT

MODEL PERFECT   SPROAT   LIMERICK

5X SHORT

STANDARD

2X LONG

4X LONG

8X LONG

TURNED UP EYE

BALL EYE

TURNED DOWN EYE

TAPERED EYE

STRAIGHT OR RINGED EYE

LOOPED EYE

Materials

The materials described here represent those most commonly used in fly tying. Many are available through a great variety of sources, others must be purchased through more specialized fly tying materials suppliers. While these are the traditional and tested materials, one should not hesitate to experiment with other materials for this is how we progress. If you don't have some of the materials required, substitution is quite acceptable for personal flies; however, be certain the replacement material has characteristics similar to the original specified material.

THREAD — Fly tying thread is made of twisted silk or nylon. The latter is most available, and generally stronger, but does stretch slightly. Thread diameter is designated by numbers beginning with 1/0 through the smaller 8/0. Even larger threads progress from size "A" through the larger size "E". Small threads build up less bulk and weight than large threads, but are not as strong. Untwisted flat nylon threads are now commonly available in two sizes, which seem to satisfy the requirements of most fly tyers. The first type, called *Mono Cord*, is available waxed or unwaxed and is good for larger flies where strength is required. The smaller type is generally described as fine *PreWaxed Nylon* and sold under various brand names. It's recommended for all smaller flies, especially drys.

BODY MATERIALS — Are those materials produced in a form which is simply wrapped on the hook shank to create the fly body. *Tinsel* is a flat metallic colored tape, usually gold or silver, and most commonly available in fine, medium, and wide sizes. Originally constructed of thin metal, a mylar plastic tinsel is now frequently used because it doesn't have sharp edges and doesn't tarnish. Oval tinsel in similar colors and sizes is also frequently specified for bodies and ribbing. *Wool* of all sorts is used, especially on wet flies and streamers since it tends to absorb water and sinks well. Orlon, Acrylic, or Polypropylene yarns are all good and seem to float better. *Floss* is made of silk, nylon, or acetate and is used mostly for sinking flies. It is readily available in a wide variety of colors. *Spun fur* is usually rabbit fur made into a yarn in various dyed colors. It's easy to work with and has a fuzzy appearance desirable on many flies. *Chenille* of nylon or rayon is sold in many sizes and colors and is best for sinking flies. *Latex* comes in sheet form which can be cut into strips and dyed or marked various colors. It sinks rapidly and is effective on many nymph patterns.

FEATHERS — This broad category is widely used in fly tying and probably every imaginable type of feather has been tried at one time or another. *Hackle* refers to feathers from the neck of a bird, most commonly a rooster. For dry flies a long, glossy, stiff hackle is desirable whereas for wet flies a soft, dull hackle is appropriate. Hackles from grouse or partridge or other birds are often short and soft and referred to as "soft hackles". Extra long, thin hackles from the rump of a rooster are called *Saddle hackles* and are used for streamer flies and larger drys. *Quills* generally refer to the primary or secondary wing quills of any bird. Goose, duck, and turkey quills in either natural or dyed colors are commonly used for tails and wings on a variety of flies. *Tail feathers* of some birds are used, mostly turkey and ringneck pheasant. The *Crest* is the topmost feathers on the head of the bird. Golden pheasant crest feathers are frequently specified in fly patterns. *Tippets* refer to the barred feathers from the lower neck of golden and amherst pheasants. *Herl* is part of a peacock or ostrich plume which has a long flexible stem and very short barbules. Peacock herl with its metallic sheen is an important fly tying ingredient. *Maribou* was originally a soft stork feather but now refers to the long downy under-feather from turkeys. It's often a replacement for streamer wings due to its undulating motion in water. *Flank feathers* from the sides of woodduck, teal, pintail, and mallard ducks are one of the most popular fly wing materials. *Body feathers* of all descriptions are used from time to time and may be referred to as back feathers, breast feathers, or rump feathers. Best known to fly tyers are those from silver and ringneck pheasants, as well as various ducks.

TAILS — An assortment of animal tails provides the fly tyer with an inexpensive supply of materials that have the qualities of length and/or stiffness. *Bucktails*, usually from the whitetail deer species provide a readily dyed source of hair used for the "Bucktail" flies, for dry fly wings and other purposes. It's best to avoid the extremely crinkled hair. *Calftails* have a finer and more transluscent hair used frequently for dry fly wings and often substituted for bucktail. Again, avoid hair that is extremely crinkled and curled. *Squirrel tails* of either the grey or red species have a fine straight hair and are also used in dyed colors. *Minktails*, in a range of natural and dyed colors have increased in popularity as their stiff hairs have proved excellent for dry fly tails and caddis fly wings. *Woodchuck tails* are used in the same manner as minktails.

HAIR — This category refers to the stiffer hairs, from the bodies of various animals. Most body hair of some animals, specifically *deer, antelope, caribou, elk* and *moose,* is stiff and generally hollow. It's used in various ways for tails, wings, and spun bodies and heads on many flies. It is important to use the proper hair for each purpose since each skin will have hair that's soft or stiff, short or long, and coarse or fine. Guard hairs (i.e. long stiffer hair as distinguished from short soft underfur) of various animals such as *badger, grey fox,* and *woodchuck* are occasionally used for streamer or salmon fly wings.

FURS — Mostly used as a dubbing material to form bodies, furs of all types and description are a basic material for fly tyers. Various colors can be mixed and blended to provide any color tone desired. Unprocessed furs, particularly from water-dwelling animals such as *muskrat, otter,* and *beaver,* contain natural oils which makes them resistant to water absorption. Furs when washed, bleached, or dyed lose this quality. Very fine furs such as *rabbit* are easiest to work with and available in many natural and dyed colors. A medium textured fur would be *Australian possum* which combines general ease of use plus a rougher texture to often give a buggy effect. *Seal fur* is a very coarse and somewhat difficult fur to use properly; it, and its substitutes, have a sheen and transluscency which makes for a brighter fly. Fur from a *European hare's mask* goes into the popular Hare's Ear dry fly, wet fly, and nymph.

SYNTHETICS — The non-availability or expense of many materials, combined with the growing variety of nylon, acrylic, rayon, dynel, kodel, mylar, polypropylene, and many other synthetics has led to substitutes, experimentation, and frequently improvement. Leading the list of synthetics today must be the variety of *synthetic furs* on the market. These are being offered in various textures and colors selected especially for fly tyers. One must match the particular synthetic to its intended use to obtain the desired qualities. Polypropylene (Poly) as a dubbing fur is lighter than water but this advantage is offset by hook weight unless the fly has the additional support of a tail and hackle. Synthetics like this do not, however, become waterlogged and dry off when casting. Conversely, when synthetics are used on heavier wet fly hooks they tend to sink faster than natural furs. Imitation seal fur, imitation polar bear, and imitation bucktail have all proved their usefulness. *Synthetic yarns,* while already accepted in many forms are finding increased usage as technology advances. Sparkle yarn comes to us via DuPont and offers the fly tyer more light reflection. Poly yarn has been utilized for dry fly wings. *Imitation jungle cock* replaces the natural feather from the jungle fowl, a bird on the Endangered Species list. *Nylon raffia* is a straw-like material which can be used for dry fly wings or the wing cases on nymphs. The list could go on extensively but many synthetics are still experimental, while others will certainly come forth in the future.

OTHER MATERIALS — In order to add weight to flies *lead wire* in various sizes is tied onto, or wrapped around the hook shank. To help secure portions of the fly and make it more durable, a flexible *cement* such as Vinyl Cement or others is useful. It can also be applied to wing quill segments to prevent splitting. *Head Cement* or lacquer, either clear or colored is essential to coat the thread windings at the head of a fly upon completion to prevent loosening, and is also used for painted eyes. *Dubbing wax* of a semi-tacky consistency is used when making fur dubbed bodies. *Waterproof markers* in a range of colors permit instant dying of some materials or the addition of realistic markings on some flies.

7

Proportions

TRADITIONAL FLY PROPORTIONS

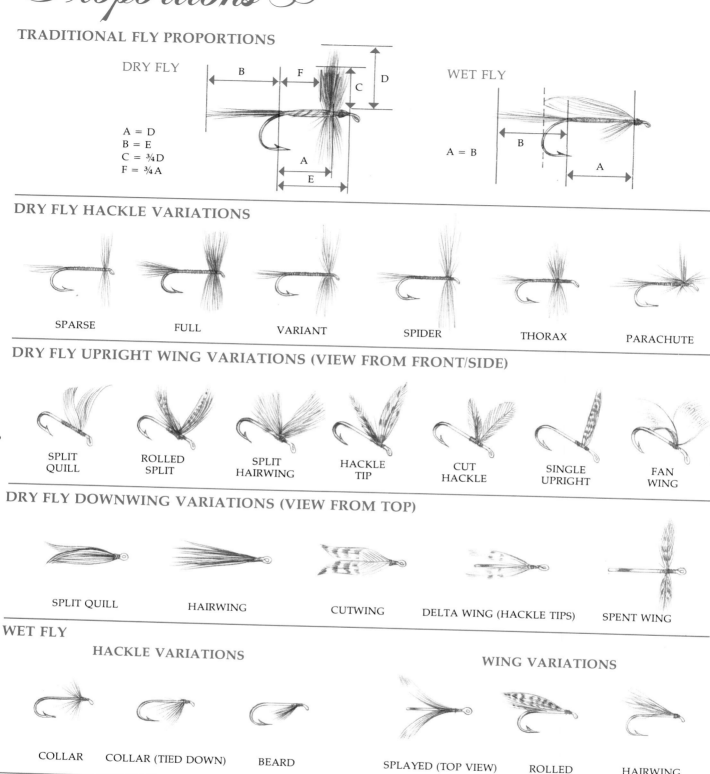

DRY FLY

A = D
B = E
C = ¾D
F = ¾A

WET FLY

A = B

DRY FLY HACKLE VARIATIONS

SPARSE   FULL   VARIANT   SPIDER   THORAX   PARACHUTE

DRY FLY UPRIGHT WING VARIATIONS (VIEW FROM FRONT/SIDE)

SPLIT QUILL   ROLLED SPLIT   SPLIT HAIRWING   HACKLE TIP   CUT HACKLE   SINGLE UPRIGHT   FAN WING

DRY FLY DOWNWING VARIATIONS (VIEW FROM TOP)

SPLIT QUILL   HAIRWING   CUTWING   DELTA WING (HACKLE TIPS)   SPENT WING

WET FLY

HACKLE VARIATIONS

COLLAR   COLLAR (TIED DOWN)   BEARD

WING VARIATIONS

SPLAYED (TOP VIEW)   ROLLED   HAIRWING

SALMON AND STEELHEAD VARIATIONS

STANDARD   REDUCED   LOW WATER

8

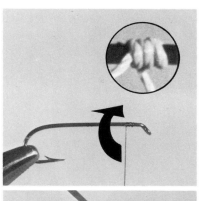

1. Place bend of hook securely in vise and starting ⅛th inch from eye of hook hold thread in left hand, bobbin in right hand, place against hook and using right hand, wrap thread over itself as shown. Cut away loose end.

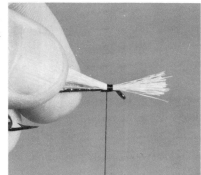

6. Take hold to the positioned bucktail with the left hand and wrap the thread 6 to 8 times tightly around the bunch, making sure not to wrap too close to the hook eye.

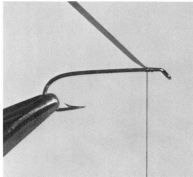

2. Cut a 4 to 6 inch piece of tinsel to a tapered end. Place the end directly over thread wraps, then secure tinsel by wrapping down with 4 or 5 turns of thread.

7. Using scissors trim the excess bucktail ends as shown.

3. Wind tinsel in close turns to rear of hook, leaving no space between turns but not overlapping.

8. Repeat steps 5, 6, and 7, using brown bucktail.

9

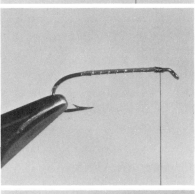

4. Wrap tinsel forward in the same manner, thus forming a smooth even body. Once tinsel is returned forward wrap down with 4 or 5 turns of thread and trim away excess tinsel.

9. Wrap down all the ends to form a neat, tapered head. Make 3 or 4 tight half hitch knots as shown and cut away thread close to head.

5. Cut a small bunch of white bucktail, align the tips to eliminate stray hairs, then holding bunch in right hand position near eye of hook to measure desired length.

10. Using a bodkin or needle apply head lacquer or cement and let dry. Repeat several times until a smooth glossy finish is achieved.

How to tie Streamers

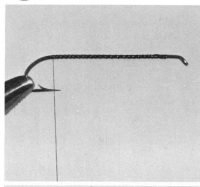

1. Provide a thread base by beginning behind hook eye and wrapping thread tightly to end of hook shank.

6. Strip a bunch of barbules from a large hackle, hold under hook with left hand, bind with thread and trim butt ends away.

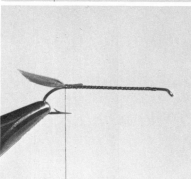

2. Select tail material and position so tail length is about same length as hook gape. Secure tail with 3 or 4 wraps of thread and cut away excess.

7. For the wing select a pair of saddle or streamer hackles, place together with concave sides facing each other, determine desired length, and strip away excess barbules.

3. Cut lengths of wool and tinsel, each about 4 to 5 inches, lay over length of shank to about ¼ inch from eye and wrap thread several times at rear, then wrap thread forward.

8. Holding hackles together in left hand, crimp the base of the feathers by placing on right index finger and pressing with right thumbnail.

4. Wrap wool tightly forward, tie down, and cut off excess.

9. Place wing on top of hook, secure with several wraps of thread, and trim away excess.

5. Spiral tinsel forward in open turns to form the rib, tie down and clip excess.

10. Position one Jungle Cock eye on each side of wing, wrap in place, and trim ends. Tie off thread using half hitches or whip finish and apply head cement.

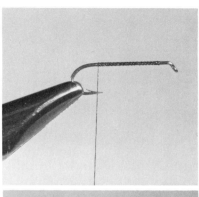

1. Start thread and wrap length of hook shank to provide a base which helps prevent materials from slipping on bare metal.

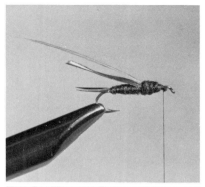

6. Move thread forward, wrap wool thickly to form thorax, tie down and cut off excess.

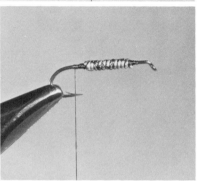

2. Cut a 3'' to 4'' length of lead wire, wrap around the center ⅔ of hook shank and secure with numerous wraps of thread.

7. Wrap hackle forward, tie down, and trim away excess.

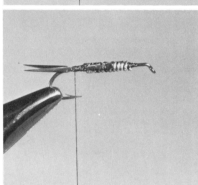

3. Select 2 stripped goose barbules or other material and tie in at rear of hook.

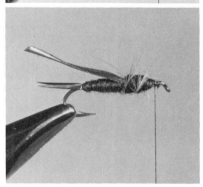

8. Using scissors trim away hackle barbules on top and bottom, leaving hackle on sides to represent legs.

11

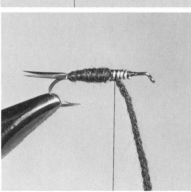

4. Attach 4'' to 5'' piece of wool or spun fur to rear ⅔ of hook shank, wrap forward to form an abdomen and tie down, but do not cut away excess.

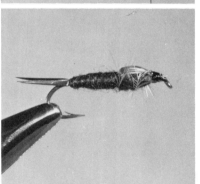

9. Fold goose quill section forward over top to form wingcase. Tie down, cut excess, wrap head, tie off, and apply head cement.

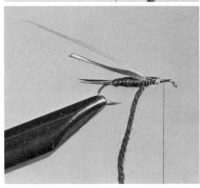

5. Attach butt end of a hackle to hook shank then attach a lacquered ¼'' wide section of goose wing quill as shown.

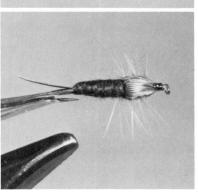

10. Top view of finished fly.

How to tie Wet Flies

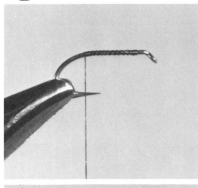

1. Begin by providing a thread foundation.

6. Pull hackle down and back as shown and wrap down with 3 or 4 turns of thread.

2. Apply tail and attach 3'' to 5'' lengths of floss and tinsel.

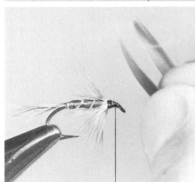

7. Select 2 wing quill segments, one each from a matched pair of duck wing quills.

3. Wrap floss forward to form a tapered body, then spiral tinsel forward in open turns to form rib. Trim away excess.

8. Holding wing tightly on top of hook shank bring thread between fingers, over wing, and down between fingers, then apply tension as you begin second similar wrap.

4. Attach soft hackle as shown and clip away excess.

9. Trim excess and wrap head. Lay a loop of separate thread as shown and wrap over 4 or 5 times with tying thread.

5. Wrap hackle 2 or 3 turns, tie down, and cut away excess.

10. Cut tying thread leaving 2'' to 3'' end which is inserted through loop. Pull on cut ends of loop thus bringing tying thread under itself. This is a whip finish knot.

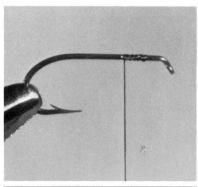

1. Begin by forming a thread base at point of wing attachment. Use a fine thread.

6. Move thread to rear and attach tail as shown.

2. Tie in section of mallard flank, tips forward, and trim away excess butt ends to a taper.

7. Apply body material or dubbing to form body.

3. Pull wing upright and make several thread turns immediately in front to hold wing up.

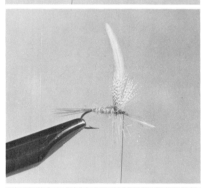

8. Pull hackles upright, then wrap first hackle mostly behind wing and tie down tip.

13

4. Divide wing into 2 equal bunches and criss cross thread through the middle.

9. Wrap second hackle, mostly in front of wing, and tie down tip.

5. Select 2 rooster hackles; strip away soft lower barbules, and attach as shown.

10. Closely cut away tips, form head with very few turns of thread, and whip finish.

Dubbing Techniques

Dubbing is probably the most useful technique in fly tying, yet it has been overlooked by many introductory books and tying classes. Dubbing involves making a "yarn" out of furs or synthetics applied to and twisted around waxed thread. Flies constructed with dubbed bodies have many advantages such as better floating or sinking qualities (depending on the materials selected), greater realism, sparkle, movement, and significantly, the ability to mix and blend different colored furs to obtain specific colors. Most difficulties result from applying too much fur, so begin by using very little.

SIMPLE TWISTED METHOD   SMOOTH LOOP METHOD   ROUGH LOOP METHOD

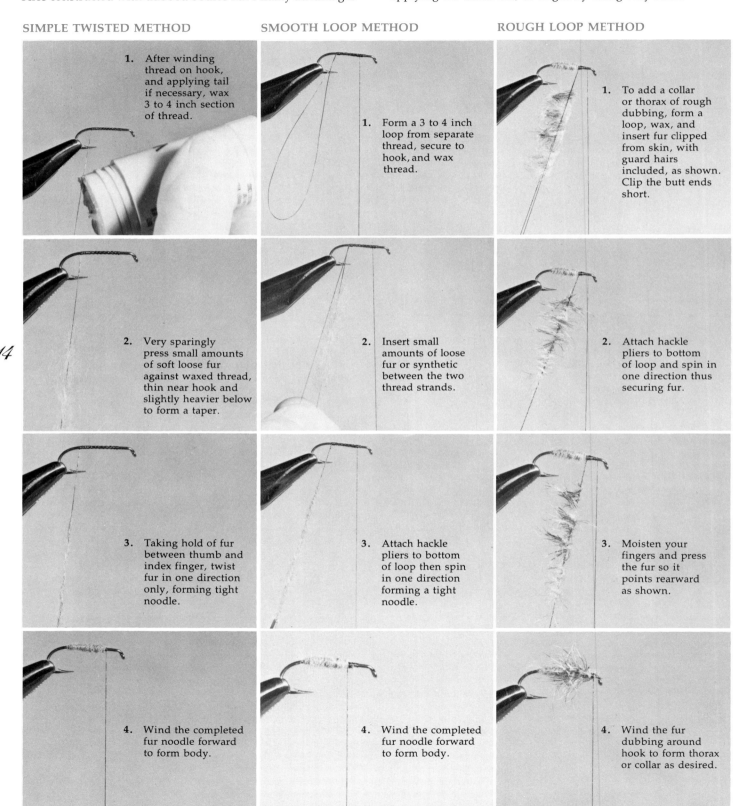

SIMPLE TWISTED METHOD

1. After winding thread on hook, and applying tail if necessary, wax 3 to 4 inch section of thread.

2. Very sparingly press small amounts of soft loose fur against waxed thread, thin near hook and slightly heavier below to form a taper.

3. Taking hold of fur between thumb and index finger, twist fur in one direction only, forming tight noodle.

4. Wind the completed fur noodle forward to form body.

SMOOTH LOOP METHOD

1. Form a 3 to 4 inch loop from separate thread, secure to hook, and wax thread.

2. Insert small amounts of loose fur or synthetic between the two thread strands.

3. Attach hackle pliers to bottom of loop then spin in one direction forming a tight noodle.

4. Wind the completed fur noodle forward to form body.

ROUGH LOOP METHOD

1. To add a collar or thorax of rough dubbing, form a loop, wax, and insert fur clipped from skin, with guard hairs included, as shown. Clip the butt ends short.

2. Attach hackle pliers to bottom of loop and spin in one direction thus securing fur.

3. Moisten your fingers and press the fur so it points rearward as shown.

4. Wind the fur dubbing around hook to form thorax or collar as desired.

Spinning Deer Body Hair

One of the techniques with which some fly tyers experience difficulty is that of spinning deer body hair such as on the Muddler Minnow, Irresitible, bass bugs, and others. The proper hair is hollow deer body hair, and each piece has dif-ferent characteristics. Fine hair works best on small flies, while coarse hair can only be used on large flies. Before attempting actual flies, first practice the following procedure on just a plain hook, it's really quite simple.

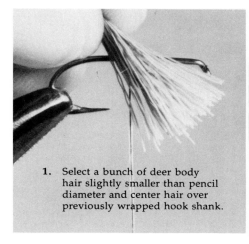

1. Select a bunch of deer body hair slightly smaller than pencil diameter and center hair over previously wrapped hook shank.

2. Still holding hair make 1½ *loose* turns of thread around center of bunch.

3. Gradually and simultaneously tighten thread, release fingers from hair, and make additional 2½ tight turns directly over previous turns.

Rotary Vise Techniques

Many professional fly tyers find that a rotating vise is more versatile than a stationary model since they can use the rotary feature for speed, smoother bodies, and for winding hackle, yet still use it as a stationary model. Additionally, materials such as floss can be easily applied direct from the spool or card and thus are less subject to handling and fraying. Instructions for use are customarily provided at the time of purchase; however, the following tips might supplement those directions.

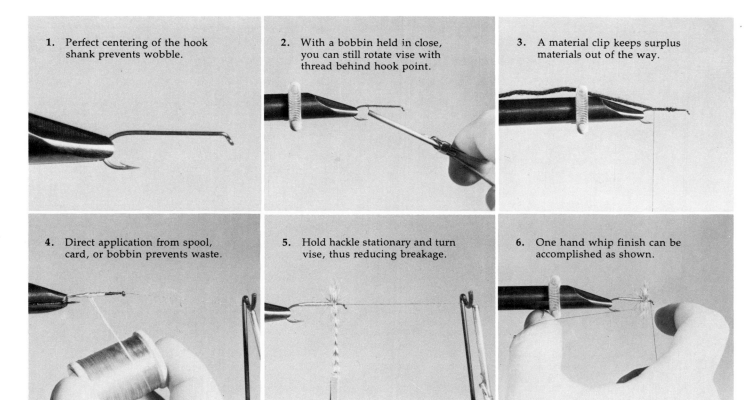

1. Perfect centering of the hook shank prevents wobble.

2. With a bobbin held in close, you can still rotate vise with thread behind hook point.

3. A material clip keeps surplus materials out of the way.

4. Direct application from spool, card, or bobbin prevents waste.

5. Hold hackle stationary and turn vise, thus reducing breakage.

6. One hand whip finish can be accomplished as shown.

Glossary

Acrylic — a synthetic yarn, tends not to absorb water
Attractor — usually a brightly colored fly which does not imitate any natural food but is simply attractive to fish
Badger — a hackle with a black center stripe, see page 19; also refers to fur from animal of the same name
Barb — part of a hook; see page 5
Barbless — a hook without a barb
Barbule — individual fiber from any feather
Barred — feather with parallel dark markings across width
Bend — see description of hooks, page 5
Beard — a style of applying throat hackle, see page 8
Bobbin — tool used to hold tying thread, see page 4
Bobbin Threader — tool to start thread through bobbin tube
Bodkin — a needle-like tool with handle, see page 4
Braided Tinsel — mylar braided around large cotton cord
Bucktail — hair from tail of deer; also a style of fly which uses bucktail as principal material
Butt — a part of fly, see page 8; also the ends of hair or feathers nearest the skin
Caddis Fly — type of common aquatic insect important to anglers, holds wings down over body
Caddis Hook — shaped hook to tie caddis larva and pupa imitations, sometimes called English Bait Hook
Cement — also called head cement or head lacquer, used to secure, preserve, and finish thread windings at head of fly
Collar — hackle or hair, wound as throat, see page 8
Covert — another term for wingcase on nymphs
Cree — a hackle of mixed white, brown, and grey markings
Crest — feather from top/back of pheasant neck
Cut Wing — hackle or breast feather cut to shape of wing
Delta Wing — style of downwing fly, see page 8
Dry Fly — artificial fly which floats upon water surface
Dubbing — a technique of applying fur; also refers to the fur itself, see page 14
Dun — see color plates; also first stage of adult mayfly
Egg Sack — imitates eggs found at rear of female insect
Emerger — an insect in the process of changing from nymph or pupa to adult
Embossed Tinsel — tinsel with reflective indentations
Eye — part of a hook, see page 5
Fanwing — style of dry fly wing using fan shaped breast feathers, see page 8
Flank — the side of a bird or duck
Floating Yarn — a polypropylene yarn
Flybody Hook — a hook style with a wire pointing rearward, used to make extended mayfly bodies
Furnace — a brown hackle with black center stripe
Gape — part of a hook measurement, see page 5
Gills — breathing parts of nymphs, usually on abdomen
Guard Hair — stiffer, longer hairs on skin of furbearers
Hackle — feather from neck or back of bird, most frequently from rooster neck unless otherwise specified
Hackle Pliers — a tool used to grip hackle, see page 4
Hair Stacker — tool used to align hair tips, see page 5
Hairwing — a fly using any of various hairs for wing
Halfhitch — the simplest knot used to secure thread
Hen — a female chicken, pheasant, or duck
Herl — short fibers on stem of peacock or ostrich plume
Horns — part of some classic salmon flies, tied on top side of wings
Hot Colors — colors with high fluorescent intensity in sunlight
Jungle Cock — endangered wild fowl from Asia; imitations of its neck feathers (eyes) now in use
Keel Hook — a hook style designed to be weedless
Lacquer — a head cement, usually offered in colors
Larva — first immature stage of insects having a complete life cycle, eg. caddis fly. See also pupa and nymph
Latex — thin flat rubber sheets, usually tan or dyed

Limerick — a style of hook, see page 5
Loop Eye — style of hook eye, see page 5
Married — procedure whereby wing quill segments of same curvature are placed together edgewise
Material Bobbin — tool to dispense spooled materials
Mayfly — a family of insects common in freshwater, of significant importance to anglers
Midge — commonly refers to very small two-winged insects
Model Perfect — a style of hook, see page 5
Monocord — a flat, untwisted nylon thread
Monofilament — single strand, clear nylon fishing line
Mylar — flat metallic colored plastic ribbon or tape, used as a nontarnishing tinsel
Neck — the complete skin with hackle feathers from chicken, most frequently a rooster
Nymph — immature aquatic first stage of insects with incomplete life cycle. Longevity from 1 to 3 years
Oval Tinsel — a tinsel wrapped around a cotton thread
Palmer — hackle wrapped over body of fly
Pantone — a brand name of colored waterproof markers
Parachute — style of applying dry fly hackle, see page 8
Polypropylene — a synthetic material, lighter than water
Prewaxed — thread waxed at factory
Pupa — the second stage in the life cycle of insects having a complete life cycle; see also larva and nymph
Quill — commonly refers to feathers from wing of bird; also the stem of any feather
Reduced — a fly reduced in size from standard, often with the elimination of non-essential materials; see page 8
Rotary Vise — vise which revolves hook on center, thereby reducing amount of arm and hand motion required
Saddle — the rear back portion of a chicken
Sculpin — a common bottom dwelling bait fish
Shank — part of a hook, see page 5
Shellback — fly with material pulled over top of body thus forming a back
Smelt — a small bait fish common in the Northeast
Soft Hackle — a short, soft, webby hackle for wet flies, usually hen, partridge, or grouse hackle
Sparse — indicates materials applied very sparingly
Spent Wing — a downwing style, see page 8
Spinner — last stage of adult mayfly life cycle
Splayed — position of wings or tail when they are set to each side in a "V" shape
Split Bead — hollow metal bead, split open on one side
Sproat — a style of hook, see page 5
Spun Fur — fur, usually rabbit, made into yarn
Stem — the center supporting quill of any feather
Stone Fly — a family of large aquatic insects, the nymph is of great importance to anglers
Streamer — type of fly designed to imitate small fish, usually made of feathers
Stripped — feather from which barbules have been removed
Tandem — two hooks, one trailing the other, connected by monofilament or wire
Tinsel — metal or metallic plastic ribbon-like material
Tippet — pheasant feather from lower neck and upper back
Underfur — soft fur nearest skin, shorter than guard hair
Upright — a style of wing, see page 8
Variant — a style of dry fly hackle, see page 8; also used to describe multicolored necks
Vinyl Cement — a very adhesive thin cement
Web — the soft, dull, webby lower center portion of hackle, undesirable for dry flys because it absorbs water
Weighted — a fly with lead wire wrapped or tied on shank
Wet Fly — a traditional style of fly that sinks in water
Whip Finish — the best finish knot for flies, see page 12

16

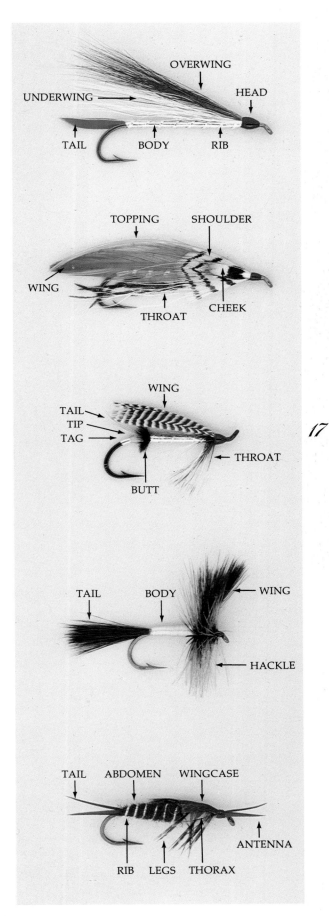

BUCKTAIL
(BROWN AND WHITE)

- OVERWING
- UNDERWING
- HEAD
- TAIL
- BODY
- RIB

STREAMER
(GREEN GHOST)

- TOPPING
- SHOULDER
- WING
- THROAT
- CHEEK

WET
(SILVER GREY)

- WING
- TAIL
- TIP
- TAG
- THROAT
- BUTT

DRY
(BLACK WULFF)

- TAIL
- BODY
- WING
- HACKLE

NYMPH
(SALMON STONE)

- TAIL
- ABDOMEN
- WINGCASE
- ANTENNA
- RIB
- LEGS
- THORAX

17

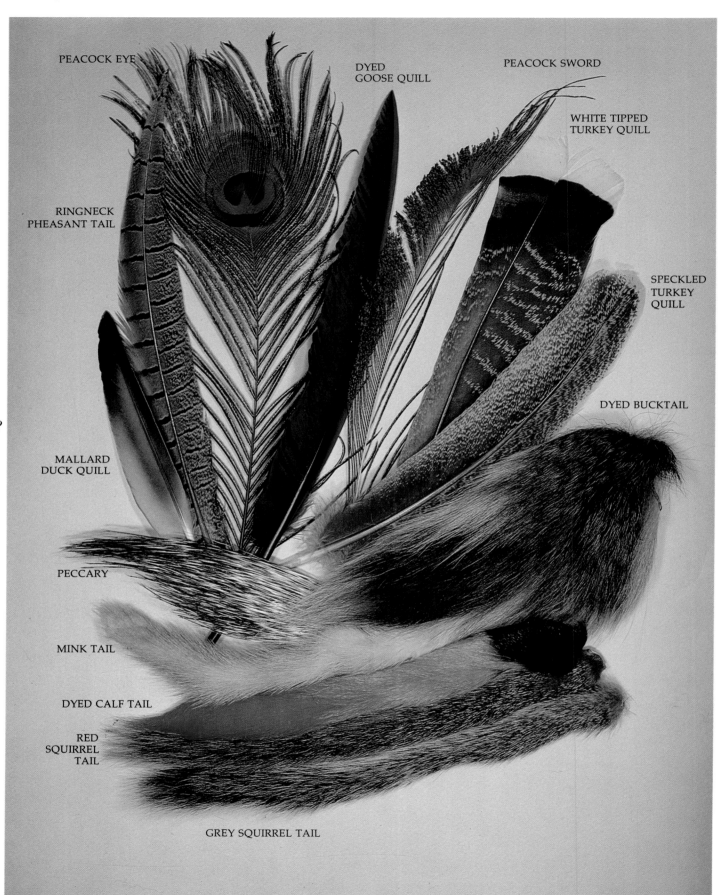

PEACOCK EYE

DYED
GOOSE QUILL

PEACOCK SWORD

WHITE TIPPED
TURKEY QUILL

RINGNECK
PHEASANT TAIL

SPECKLED
TURKEY
QUILL

DYED BUCKTAIL

MALLARD
DUCK QUILL

PECCARY

MINK TAIL

DYED CALF TAIL

RED
SQUIRREL
TAIL

GREY SQUIRREL TAIL

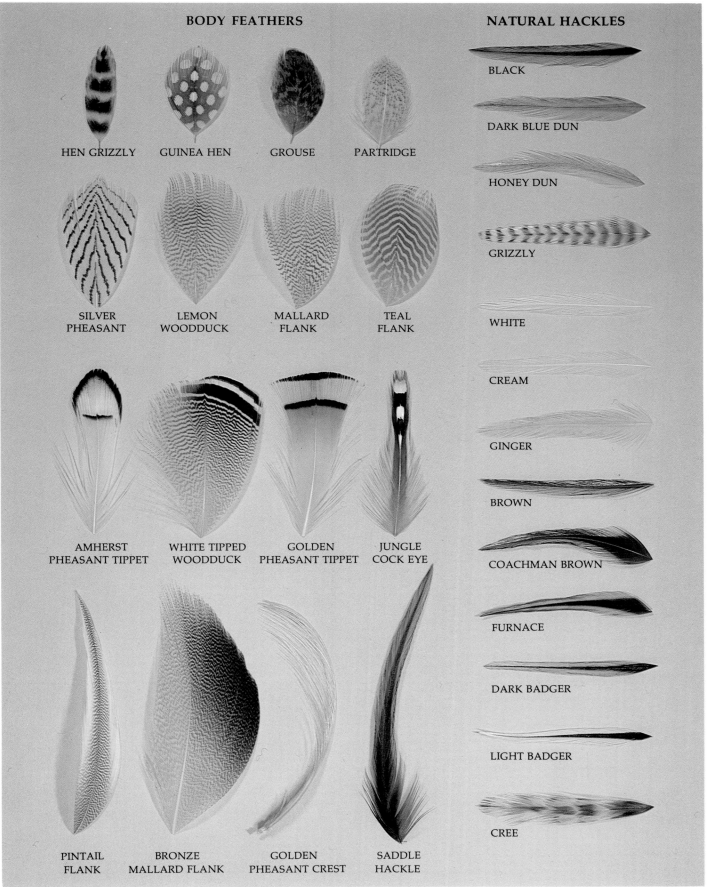

BODY FEATHERS

HEN GRIZZLY GUINEA HEN GROUSE PARTRIDGE

SILVER PHEASANT LEMON WOODDUCK MALLARD FLANK TEAL FLANK

AMHERST PHEASANT TIPPET WHITE TIPPED WOODDUCK GOLDEN PHEASANT TIPPET JUNGLE COCK EYE

PINTAIL FLANK BRONZE MALLARD FLANK GOLDEN PHEASANT CREST SADDLE HACKLE

NATURAL HACKLES

BLACK

DARK BLUE DUN

HONEY DUN

GRIZZLY

WHITE

CREAM

GINGER

BROWN

COACHMAN BROWN

FURNACE

DARK BADGER

LIGHT BADGER

CREE

19

Color Guide

This color guide is designed to show those colors most referred to by fly tyers and fly tying books. The particular shades used here were selected from hundreds of color hues on a consensus basis by a team of several long experienced tyers, and thus present an average interpretation. It might be noted that only rarely was there total agreement on a color. Natural furs and feathers have properties such as translucency and blended tones we cannot reproduce in flat color chips, so some judgement should be exercised when making a direct comparison. The relative value of these colors should prove very useful in selecting materials, particularly to beginning tyers.

20

LIGHT BLUE DUN GREY	CREAM	DARK BROWN	ORANGE	PINK	INSECT GREEN
BLUE DUN GREY	CREAM GINGER	COACHMAN BROWN	BURNT ORANGE	LIGHT BLUE	SUPERVISOR GREEN
DARK BLUE DUN GREY	LIGHT GINGER	RED BROWN	SCARLET	BLUE	LIGHT OLIVE
HONEY DUN	GINGER	LIGHT YELLOW	RED	TEAL BLUE	OLIVE
DUN	DARK GINGER	YELLOW	MAGENTA	KINGFISHER BLUE	DARK OLIVE
RUSTY DUN	TAN	GOLDEN YELLOW	CLARET	DARK GREEN	GOLD OLIVE
IRON DUN	LIGHT BROWN	AMBER	PURPLE	GREEN	BROWN OLIVE
BLACK	BROWN	CINNAMON	CERISE	GRASS GREEN	GREEN OLIVE

HOOK — *Mustad 94840 or similar ; sizes 10 to 20*
THREAD — *Black*
TAIL — *Mixed grizzly and brown hackle barbules*
BODY — *Grey muskrat underfur*
WING — *Grizzly hackle tips*
HACKLE — *Mixed grizzly and brown*
COMMENT — *The Adams is probably the most popular dry fly in use today. In a variety of sizes, it belongs in everyone's fly box.*

HOOK — *Mustad 94840 or similar ; sizes 10 to 16*
THREAD — *Brown*
TAIL — *Brown hackle barbules*
BODY — *Hackle tied in at rear of hook and closely wound forward. Often more than one hackle is required. At front place 2 or 3 turns of white hackle to make fly more visible.*
COMMENT — *A high floating fly, the bivisible is particularly good in fast water. Other popular colors are blue dun, ginger, black and badger, all with white up front.*

HOOK — *Mustad 94840 or similar ; sizes 10 to 18*
THREAD — *Black*
TAIL — *Black hackle barbules*
BODY — *Black dubbed fur*
WING — *Slate grey mallard wing quill sections*
HACKLE — *Black*
COMMENT — *A popular dark fly which has many variations. It is very good as a Midge pattern tied without wings in sizes 20 to 24.*

HOOK — *Mustad 94840 or similar ; sizes 14 to 22*
THREAD — *Olive*
TAIL — *Dark blue dun hackle barbules*
BODY — *Brown olive dubbed fur*
WING — *Dark blue dun hackle points*
HACKLE — *Dark blue dun*
COMMENT — *Several mayfly species in the olive group have similar coloration, but sizes will vary considerably. Some anglers prefer a body color of a blend of 1/3 olive and 2/3 brown rabbit.*

HOOK — *Mustad 94840 or similar ; sizes 12 to 20*
THREAD — *Yellow*
TAIL — *Cream hackle barbules*
BODY — *Stem from cream hackle, well soaked, small end tied in at rear and wrapped forward.*
WING — *None*
HACKLE — *Cream – all variants are tied with hackle one size larger than standard. See page 8.*

ADAMS

BIVISIBLE (BROWN)

BLACK GNAT

BLUE WINGED OLIVE

CREAM VARIANT

21

FAN WING ROYAL COACHMAN

HOOK — *Mustad 94840 or similar ; sizes 8 to 14.*
THREAD — *Black*
TAIL — *Coachman brown hackle barbules*
BODY — *Rear 1/4 peacock herl, middle 1/2 red floss, front 1/4 peacock herl.*
WING — *2 white woodduck breast feathers*
HACKLE — *Coachman brown*

GREEN DRAKE (FEMALE)

HOOK — *Mustad 94831 (2x long) ; sizes 6-8-10*
THREAD — *Olive*
TAIL — *Ginger hackle barbules*
BODY — *Dubbed fur mixture of 1/2 pale yellow rabbit with 1/2 tan red fox fur*
RIB — *Thin strand of medium brown floss twisted into a thread and wrapped as rib.*
WING — *Woodduck flank*
HACKLE — *Mixed grizzly, ginger, and pale olive hackles*
COMMENT — *Can also be tied slightly darker to represent male green drake.*

GREY FOX

HOOK — *Mustad 94840 or similar ; sizes 12 to 18*
THREAD — *Pale yellow*
TAIL — *Ginger hackle barbules*
BODY — *Tan colored fur from red fox*
WING — *Mallard flank*
HACKLE — *Mixed light ginger and light grizzly*

HENDRICKSON

HOOK — *Mustad 94840 or similar ; sizes 12 and 14*
THREAD — *Yellow*
TAIL — *Medium blue dun*
BODY — *Pinkish urine burned red fox fur*
WING — *Woodduck flank*
HACKLE — *Medium blue dun*

LIGHT CAHILL

HOOK — *Mustad 94840 or similar ; sizes 12 and 14*
THREAD — *Yellow*
TAIL — *Light ginger hackle barbules*
BODY — *Cream belly fur from red fox*
WING — *Woodduck flank*
HACKLE — *Light ginger to cream ginger*
COMMENT — *Like the Black Gnat, when tied in sizes 20 to 24, the light cahill makes a good midge pattern.*

HOOK — *Mustad 94840 or similar ; sizes 10 and 12*
THREAD — *Orange*
TAIL — *Ginger hackle barbules*
BODY — *Tan colored fur from red fox*
WING — *Woodduck flank*
HACKLE — *Mixed dark ginger and dark grizzly*

MARCH BROWN

HOOK — *Mustad 94840 or similar ; sizes 12 to 18*
THREAD — *Black*
TAIL — *Grizzly hackle barbules*
BODY — *Moose mane, one light strand and one dark strand wrapped together*
WING — *Grizzly hackle tips*
HACKLE — *Grizzly*
COMMENT — *For durability, coat the body with lacquer.*

MOSQUITO

HOOK — *Mustad 94840 or similar ; sizes 12 to 18*
THREAD — *Olive*
TAIL — *Medium blue dun*
BODY — *Quill section from lower part of peacock eye, stripped of herl and wrapped on to make segmented body*
WING — *Woodduck flank*
HACKLE — *Medium blue dun*
COMMENT — *Often this is the first mayfly to appear at streamside in the early spring.*

QUILL GORDON

23

HOOK — *Mustad 94840 or similar ; sizes 10 to 18*
THREAD — *Olive*
TAIL — *Medium blue dun hackle barbules*
BODY — *Well soaked quill (stem) from reddish-brown hackle which has been stripped of barbules*
WING — *Woodduck flank*
HACKLE — *Medium blue dun*
COMMENT — *An excellent fly representing several mayfly species. Can be converted to a spinner by clipping hackle top and bottom.*

RED QUILL

HOOK — *Mustad 94838 or 9523 ; sizes 12 to 20*
THREAD — *Black*
TAIL — *Badger hackle barbules*
HACKLE — *Oversize stiff badger hackle*
COMMENT — *Spiders are popular low water flies ; also tied in blue dun, black, brown and light ginger.*

SPIDER (BADGER)

AUSABLE WULFF

HOOK — *Mustad 7957B or 9671 ; sizes 8 to 16*
THREAD — *Flourescent red*
TAIL — *Woodchuck tail*
BODY — *Cinnamon-rusty orange Australian possum fur dubbing.*
WING — *White calf tail*
HACKLE — *Mixed brown and grizzly*

BIRDS STONEFLY

HOOK — *Mustad 9672 or 9671 ; sizes 4 to 10*
THREAD — *Orange*
TAIL — *2 strands of dark peccary*
BODY — *Burnt orange floss with bands of brown hackle, clipped short*
WING — *Brown bucktail fanned out flat over body*
HACKLE — *Furnace wrapped on, then flattened on top and bottom, clipped on sides and lacquered in place.*
ANTENNA — *2 strands dark peccary*
COMMENT — *May also be tied with a yellow body.*

GREY RIFFLE

HOOK — *Mustad 9671 or similar ; sizes 10 to 16*
THREAD — *Black*
TAIL — *White calftail*
BODY — *Grey muskrat dubbing*
WING — *White calftail, slightly long*
HACKLE — *Medium blue dun tied quite heavy*
COMMENT — *This is an excellent fly with high visibility for late evening fishing. The riffle fly series includes grizzly, brown, ginger, cream and black, all with white wing and tail.*

GREY WULFF

HOOK — *Mustad 7957B or 9671 ; sizes 8 to 16*
THREAD — *Black*
TAIL — *Brown bucktail or elk*
BODY — *Bluish-grey spun fur or muskrat dubbing*
WING — *Brown bucktail or elk*
HACKLE — *Medium to dark blue dun*

GRIZZLY WULFF

HOOK — *Mustad 7957B or 9671 ; sizes 8 to 16*
THREAD — *Black*
TAIL — *Brown bucktail or elk*
BODY — *Yellow floss or dubbed fur*
WING — *Brown bucktail*
HACKLE — *Mixed grizzly and brown*
COMMENT — *If floss is used for body, it should be lacquered after being wound in place.*

24

HOOK — *Mustad 7957B or 9671 ; sizes 6 to 14*
THREAD — *Yellow*
TAIL — *Light elk*
BODY — *Over rear 60% of shank tie in clump of light elk with tips extending rearward past end of tail. Wrap thread tightly forward to provide body color, then fold elk hair over back and tie down.*
WING — *Light elk*
HACKLE — *Mixed grizzly and brown*
COMMENT — *Also known as the Goofus Bug, this fly is tied with red, orange, green and fluorescent green bodies with dark elk being used with dark bodies.*

HOOK — *Mustad 7957B or 9671 ; sizes 8 to 14*
THREAD — *Black*
TAIL — *Brown bucktail or elk*
BODY — *Spun grey-brown deer body hair clipped to shape shown.*
WING — *Brown bucktail or elk*
HACKLE — *Medium to dark blue dun tied heavy*
COMMENT — *This is a good floating fly, but most beginning fly tyers find the construction difficult. Is also tied with the colors of an Adams.*

HOOK — *Mustad 7957B or 9671 ; sizes 8 to 16*
THREAD — *Black*
TAIL — *Brown bucktail or elk*
BODY — *Rear 1/4 peacock herl, mid 1/2 red floss, front 1/4 peacock herl*
WING — *White calftail or bucktail*
HACKLE — *Coachman brown*

HOOK — *Mustad 7957B or 9671 ; sizes 8 to 14*
THREAD — *Brown*
TAIL — *Dark elk*
BODY — *Red wool or dubbing*
RIB — *Flat silver tinsel*
WING — *Red squirrel tail extending to middle of tail*
HACKLE — *Reddish brown*
COMMENT — *One of many Trude patterns which are of similar construction ; tied in various colors, usually adaptations of standard dry flies, such as Royal Coachman, Rio Grande King, Black Gnat, etc.*

HOOK — *Mustad 7957B or 9671 ; sizes 8 to 16*
THREAD — *Black*
TAIL — *White bucktail or other stiff hair*
BODY — *Cream spun fur or dubbing*
WING — *White bucktail or other stiff hair*
HACKLE — *Light badger*

HUMPY

IRRESISTIBLE

ROYAL WULFF

TRUDE (RED)

WHITE WULFF

25

BUCKTAIL CADDIS (YELLOW)

HOOK — *Mustad 7957B or 9671 ; sizes 8 to 14*
THREAD — *Brown*
TAIL — *Brown hackle fibers, tied short*
BODY — *Yellow spun fur or floating yarn*
RIB — *Brown hackle palmered over body*
WING — *Brown bucktail taken from near base of tail*
HACKLE — *Brown*
COMMENT — *Also tied with orange or green body*

COLORADO KING (LIGHT)

HOOK — *Mustad 94840 or similar ; sizes 8 to 18*
THREAD — *Black*
TAIL — *2 strands of peccary, one tied at each side and spread wide for stability. Before applying tail, tie in a small ball of dubbing at rear of hook – this helps spread tail.*
BODY — *Dubbed yellow rabbit*
HACKLE — *Grizzly palmered over body*
WING — *Light elk*
COMMENT — *A successful pattern also tied in darker color combinations*

HAIRWING CADDIS

HOOK — *Mustad 94840 or similar ; sizes 10 to 18*
THREAD — *Black*
BODY — *Mixed olive and brown dubbing*
WING — *Dark grey mink tail guard hairs tied in three bunches on top and slightly to each side*
HACKLE — *Dark blue dun*
COMMENT — *This is a basic hairwing caddis construction which can be adapted to match actual specimens. Other combinations include all black, olive body and brown wing, light olive/grey body and tan wing, yellow/brown body and cream/tan wing, and grey/brown body and wing.*

HENRYVILLE SPECIAL

HOOK — *Mustad 94840 or similar ; sizes 12 to 20*
THREAD — *Brown*
TAIL — *None*
BODY — *Olive dubbing ribbed with grizzly hackle, the barbules of which should not extend much past the hook point.*
WING — *Underwing of 4 or 5 strands of barred woodduck, which extend beyond hook bend. Overwing of sections of mallard wing quill tied tent-like over body.*
HACKLE — *Dark ginger tied sparse*
COMMENT — *Probably the best all-around caddis imitation, fished both dry and wet.*

WOODCHUCK CADDIS

HOOK — *Mustad 9671 or similar ; sizes 10 to 16*
THREAD — *Brown*
TAIL — *2 or 3 brown elk hairs tied in and spread on each side*
BODY — *Woodchuck underfur dubbing*
RIB — *Red-grizzly hackle*
WING — *Well marked woodchuck tail*
HACKLE — *Red-grizzly*

HOOK — *Mustad 79580 ; sizes 6 and 8*
THREAD — *Yellow*
TAIL — *Brown minktail guard hairs split to each side*
BODY — *Creamy yellow dubbing*
WING — *Single upright wing of medium greyish deer body hair*
HACKLE — *A few turns medium blue dun fore and aft of wing (optional)*
COMMENT — *The Compara-dun style utilizes light wire hooks, splayed tails, dubbed bodies, and deer hair or deer mask hair for wings. Eight standard compara-dun patterns, ranging from white to black, seem to generally simulate the majority of mayfly species. The Hexagenia is of importance in the Midwest and parts of the Northeast.*

HOOK — *Mustad 94833 ; sizes 12 to 22*
THREAD — *Brown*
TAIL — *Grey hackle barbules or minktail guard hairs, split to each side*
BODY — *Reddish brown dubbed fur or polypropylene*
WING — *Light grey hen hackle tips tied spent wing*
COMMENT — *Hen spinners are also tied in combinations of dun/yellow, dun/cream, and white/black to match the naturals. Hen wings can be replaced by wrapped dry fly hackle clipped off on top and bottom.*

HOOK — *Mustad 94833 ; sizes 12 to 24*
THREAD — *Brown*
TAIL — *Ginger hackle barbules, split to each side*
BODY — *Tan dubbed fur or polypropylene*
WING — *Dark grey mallard wing quill sections*
COMMENT — *Some practice may be necessary to properly set wings. Other color combinations are light grey/yellow, light grey/light olive, and dark grey/medium olive.*

HOOK — *Mustad 94833 ; sizes 16 to 24*
THREAD — *Olive*
TAIL — *Grey hackle barbules, split to each side*
BODY — *Olive dubbed fur or polyprophlene*
WING — *Single upright wing of grey hackle barbules*
HACKLE — *A few turns of medium blue dun (optional)*
COMMENT — *There are 10 representative patterns of para-duns, ranging from slate/brown to cream/yellow, designed to match most maylies. On larger sizes deer or elk hair is used for wing.*

HOOK — *Mustad 94842 or 94859 ; sizes 22 to 26*
THREAD — *White*
TAIL — *3 separated light grey minktail fibers (tied long)*
BODY — *White tying thread*
THORAX — *Black dubbed fur or polypropylene*
WING — *White polypropylene yarn tied spent wing style*
COMMENT — *Although commonly called Caenis, this is actually a Tricorythodes imitation.*

COMPARADUN (HEXAGENIA)

HEN SPINNER
(DUN/BROWN)

NO HACKLE
(SLATE/TAN)

PARADUN
(GREY/OLIVE)

POLYWING SPINNER
(CAENIS)

27

BLUE DUN

HOOK — *Mustad 3906 or similar ; sizes 8 to 14*
THREAD — *Grey*
TAIL — *Medium blue dun hackle barbules*
BODY — *Grey dubbing or spun fur*
HACKLE — *Medium blue dun*
WING — *Grey duck wing quill segments.*
COMMENT — *An old standard wet fly.*

DARK CAHILL

HOOK — *Mustad 3906 or similar ; sizes 10 to 16*
THREAD — *Black*
TAIL — *Woodduck flank barbules*
BODY — *Grey dubbing or spun fur*
HACKLE — *Brown*
WING — *Woodduck flank*

28

GREY HACKLE

HOOK — *Mustad 3906 or similar ; sizes 8 to 16*
THREAD — *Black*
TAIL — *Red hackle barbules (optional)*
BODY — *Peacock herl*
WING — *None*
HACKLE — *Grizzly*
COMMENT — *A simple yet effective wet fly. A similar fly, the Brown Hackle, is identical except brown hackle replaces the grizzly.*

GRIZZLY KING

HOOK — *Mustad 3906 or similar ; sizes 10 to 16*
THREAD — *Black*
TAIL — *Red hackle barbules or red duck quill strip*
BODY — *Bright green floss*
RIB — *Flat gold tinsel*
HACKLE — *Grizzly*
WING — *Mallard flank*

HENDRICKSON EMERGER

HOOK — *Mustad 3906B or similar ; sizes 12 and 14*
THREAD — *Olive*
TAIL — *Woodduck flank barbules, slightly shorter than body*
BODY — *Dark reddish brown dubbing.*
WING — *Dark grey hen hackle tips, 2/3 body length*
LEGS — *Woodduck flank barbules, tied short*

HOOK — *Mustad 3906 or similar ; sizes 12 to 18*
THREAD — *Red*
TAIL — *Honey dun hackle barbules*
BODY — *Mole fur or dark muskrat dubbed onto red thread. At rear of body, leave some of red showing.*
HACKLE — *Honey dun, preferably with brownish outside edges, collar slightly tied back.*
COMMENT — *A Leisenring pattern which is very effective.*

HOOK — *Mustad 3906 or similar ; sizes 10 to 16*
THREAD — *Black*
TAG — *Flat gold tinsel*
BODY — *Peacock herl*
HACKLE — *Coachman brown*
WING — *Dark grey duck wing quill segments*

HOOK — *Mustad 3906 or similar ; sizes 8 to 14*
THREAD — *Black*
TAIL — *Mixed red and white hackle barbules*
BODY — *Yellow floss*
RIB — *Flat gold tinsel*
WING — *Married sections of red and white duck wing quills, red on top*
HACKLE — *Mixed red and white*
COMMENT — *Still a popular and colorful attractor fly.*

HOOK — *Mustad 3906 or similar ; sizes 10 to 16*
THREAD — *Orange*
TAIL — *None*
BODY — *Rear 2/3rd orange floss, front 1/3rd mixed black and brown hare's mask dubbing*
HACKLE — *Brown partridge*
COMMENT — *This is an example of the "soft-hackled" fly recommended by many anglers. Also popular with green or yellow body, matching thread, and brown or grey partridge hackle.*

HOOK — *Mustad 9672 or similar ; sizes 8 to 14*
THREAD — *Black*
TAIL — *Brown hackle barbules*
BODY — *Peacock herl*
RIB — *Brown hackle palmered over body*
WING — *Grey squirrel tail*
HEAD — *Peacock herl*

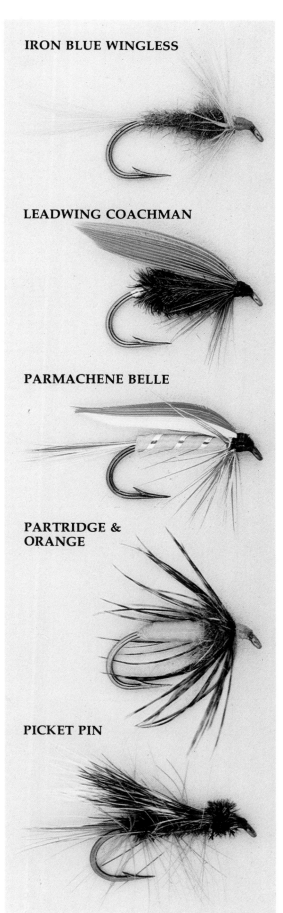

IRON BLUE WINGLESS

LEADWING COACHMAN

PARMACHENE BELLE

PARTRIDGE & ORANGE

PICKET PIN

29

PROFESSOR

HOOK — *Mustad 3906 or similar ; sizes 8 to 14*
THREAD — *Black*
TAIL — *Red hackle barbules or red duck quill segment*
BODY — *Yellow floss*
RIB — *Flat gold tinsel*
HACKLE — *Brown*
WING — *Mallard flank*

QUILL GORDON

HOOK — *Mustad 3906 or similar ; sizes 12 to 18*
THREAD — *Olive*
TAIL — *Woodduck flank barbules*
BODY — *Stripped peacock quill*
RIB — *Fine gold wire*
WING — *Woodduck flank*
HACKLE — *Dark blue dun*

RENEGADE

HOOK — *Mustad 3906 or similar ; sizes 6 to 18*
THREAD — *Black*
TAG — *Flat gold tinsel*
REAR HACKLE — *Brown*
BODY — *Peacock herl reinforced by overwrap of fine gold wire*
FRONT HACKLE — *White*
COMMENT — *An extremely popular Rocky Mountains pattern, very often tied as a dry fly ; also often weighted.*

RIO GRANDE KING

HOOK — *Mustad 3906 or similar ; sizes 8 to 14*
THREAD — *Black*
TAIL — *Yellow hackle barbules*
BODY — *Black chenille*
HACKLE — *Yellow*
WING — *White duck quill segments, splayed.*

WOOLY WORM (BLACK)

HOOK — *Mustad 9671, 9672 or 79580 ; sizes 4 to 12*
THREAD — *Black*
TAIL — *Short red wool*
BODY — *Black chenille*
RIB — *Oval silver tinsel (optional)*
HACKLE — *Grizzly saddle hackle palmered over body*
COMMENT — *Also popular with yellow, olive, or brown body, with grizzly or brown hackle. Tied on various length hooks, and frequently weighted.*

30

HOOK — *Mustad 9672 or similar ; sizes 6 to 12*
THREAD — *Black*
TAIL — *Muskrat fur with guard hairs left in*
BODY — *Muskrat fur using loop dubbing twisted tight to give segmented effect*
THORAX — *Thick muskrat fur with guard hairs tied pointing rearward*
HEAD — *Black ostrich herl*

HOOK — *Mustad 3906B or 9671 ; sizes 6 to 18*
THREAD — *Brown*
TAIL — *4 or 5 strands woodduck flank*
BODY — *Dubbing mixture of black, brown and grey fur from base of ears of English Hare's mask. Make thick toward thorax.*
RIB — *Fine oval gold, tinsel*
WINGCASE — *Woodduck flank feather tied in at head to extend over thorax and clipped short*
LEGS — *Fur from thorax picked out on each side with bodkin*
COMMENT — *For many anglers this is the best all around nymph ; often weighted.*

HOOK — *Mustad 3906 or similar ; sizes 8 to 14*
THREAD — *Tan*
TAIL — *Few short strands brown grouse hackle*
BODY — *Rough dubbed otter fur*
LEGS — *Brown grouse hackle bunch, tied in beard style*
COMMENT — *A common practice is to use olive thread if fly is weighted.*

HOOK — *Mustad 3906B or 9671 ; sizes 8 to 14*
THREAD — *Black*
TAIL — *None, or few short brown hackle barbules*
SHELLBACK — *Quill segment from cock ringneck pheasant tail or several strands of peacock herl pulled foreward over body after rib is wrapped.*
BODY — *Yellow floss tied thick*
RIB — *Peacock herl*
LEGS — *Soft brown hackle collared and tied down*

HOOK — *Mustad 9671 or 3906B ; sizes 8 to 14*
THREAD — *Black*
TAIL — *3 strands of peacock sword*
BODY — *Peacock herl tied thick*
RIB — *Oval silver tinsel*
HACKLE — *Soft brown*
WINGCASE — *Mallard breast cut short to extend 1/4th of body length*

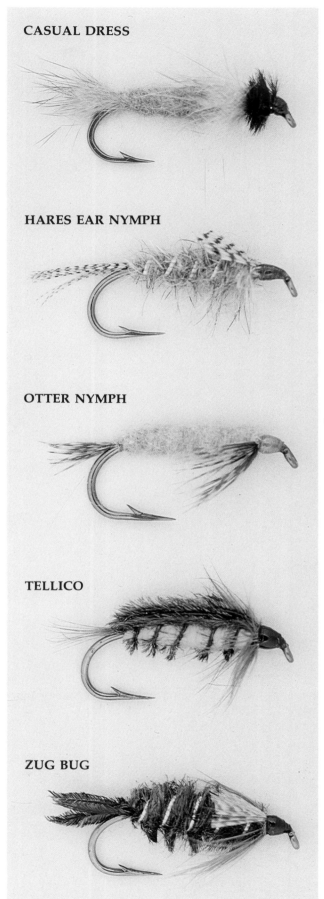

CASUAL DRESS

HARES EAR NYMPH

OTTER NYMPH

TELLICO

ZUG BUG

31

ATHERTON DARK

HOOK — *Mustad 3906B ; sizes 10 to 16*
THREAD — *Black*
TAIL — *Furnace hackle barbules*
ABDOMEN — *Equal mix of grey muskrat and claret seal fur*
RIB — *Oval gold tinsel*
WINGCASE — *Kingfisher (iridescent greenish blue) dyed goose or floss*
THORAX — *Same as abdomen*
LEGS — *Furnace hackle collared and clipped top and bottom*
COMMENT — *Atherton Light and Medium nymphs are also popular.*

COMPARA NYMPH (YELLOW-BROWN)

HOOK — *Mustad 94840, 9671 or 9672 ; sizes 4 to 18*
THREAD — *Cream*
BODY — *Yellowish brown fur blend*
LEGS — *Light ginger*
WINGCASE — *Brown goose quill section*
COMMENT — *Using same style, also tied in following color combinations:*

Thread	Body	Legs	Wingcase
Tan	red/brown	ginger	dark brown
Olive	olive/brown	dark ginger	dark grey/brown
Brown	dark brown	red brown	black

FLOATING NYMPH (YELLOW)

HOOK — *Mustad 94833 or 94831 ; sizes 10 to 20*
THREAD — *Pale yellow*
TAIL — *Pale yellow hackle barbules, tied split*
ABDOMEN — *Cream/yellow fur dubbing*
RIB — *Brown thread*
THORAX — *Same as abdomen*
LEGS — *Very short and sparse yellow pale yellow hackle, clipped top and bottom*
WING — *Large clump grey/yellow fur or polypropylene as ball on top of thorax.*
COMMENT — *This represents a style which can be tied in other colors to match the natural insects.*

MARTINEZ

HOOK — *Mustad 3906B or similar ; sizes 10 to 16*
THREAD — *Black*
TAIL — *Few strands black and white guinea hackle*
ABDOMEN — *Dubbed black seal fur*
RIB — *Fine copper tinsel*
THORAX — *Black chenille*
WINGCASE — *Bright green floss, wool, or raffia*
HACKLE — *Grey partridge*

WHIT TAN NYMPH

HOOK — *Mustad 9671 or 9672*
THREAD — *Black*
TAIL — *A few well marked barbules from hen pheasant wing quill*
ABDOMEN — *Cream tan fur dubbing blend*
RIB — *Oval gold tinsel*
WINGCASE — *Mallard hen wing quill dyed olive brown*
THORAX — *Fur, including guard hairs, from skin of grey squirrel, dubbed rough to also represent legs.*
COMMENT — *Using same tying method, other mayfly nymphs may be represented by carefully matching the proper color blends.*

HOOK — *Mustad 38941 or 9672 ; sizes 4 to 8*
THREAD — *Brown*
TAIL — *3 tan or tan/grey ostrich herl tips, 1/3 body length*
ABDOMEN — *Light cream/amber seal fur or dubbing substitute, marked on back with brown waterproof ink marker ; picked out on sides.*
THORAX — *Cream/amber fur with guard hairs, loop dubbed to also form legs.*
WINGCASE — *Brown goose quill section*

HOOK — *Mustad 3906B or 9671 ; sizes 10 and 12*
THREAD — *Brown*
TAIL — *Well marked woodduck flank barbules, 1/2 body length*
ABDOMEN — *Amber/reddish brown dubbing, picked out lightly on sides*
WINGCASE — *Dark mottled turkey tail section*
THORAX — *Same as abdomen*
LEGS — *Brown partridge or grouse hackle applied as collar and tied back before wingcase is brought forward.*

HOOK — *Mustad 38941 or 9672 ; sizes 8 and 10*
THREAD — *Brown*
TAIL — *Three peacock herl tips, 1/3 body length*
ABDOMEN — *Dark purple/brown seal fur or dubbing substitute, also thin white strip of light moose mane tied down over abdomen and wing case. Pick out fur a little on each side to represent gills.*
RIB — *Claret thread*
THORAX — *Well marked greyish guard hairs and fur from hares mask, loop dubbed to also form legs.*
WINGCASE — *Dark greyish/brown latex, cut to shape, 1/3 body length*

HOOK — *Mustad 38941 or 9672 ; sizes 10 and 12*
THREAD — *Brown*
TAIL — *Three light brown barbules from cock ringneck pheasant, 1/3 body length*
ABDOMEN — *Yellowish/brown seal fur or dubbing substitute, picked out long on sides. Also apply reddish/brown markings on back with waterproof ink marker.*
THORAX — *Yellowish/brown fur with guard hairs, loop dubbed to also form legs.*
WINGCASE — *Red/brown latex, cut to shape, 1/3 body length.*

HOOK — *Mustad 3906B or 9671 ; sizes 10 and 12*
THREAD — *Brown*
TAIL — *3 strands from cock ringneck pheasant tail, spread out*
ABDOMEN — *Dubbed mixture of amber seal fur and tan fur from red fox.*
RIB — *Brown cotton thread*
WINGCASE — *Mottled grey/brown segment from underside of ringneck pheasant tail.*
THORAX — *Same as abdomen*
LEGS — *Brown partridge hackle barbules*

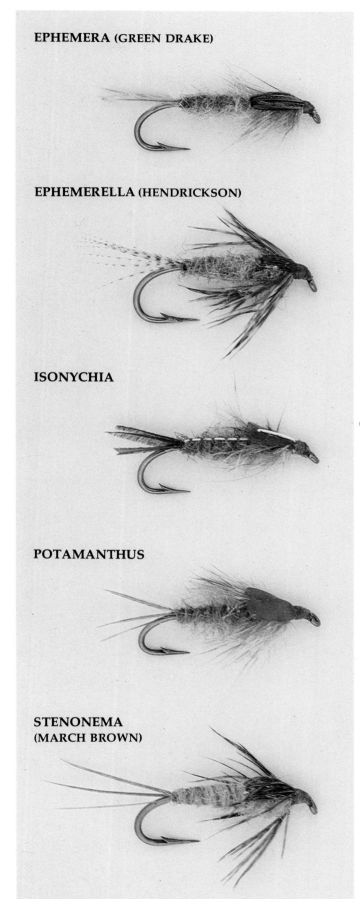

EPHEMERA (GREEN DRAKE)

EPHEMERELLA (HENDRICKSON)

ISONYCHIA

POTAMANTHUS

STENONEMA (MARCH BROWN)

33

Stonefly Nymphs

BLACK STONE

HOOK — *Mustad 9672 or 38941 ; sizes 2 to 8*
THREAD — *Black*
TAIL — *Dark brown goose quill barbules tied one on each side of abdomen*
ABDOMEN — *Weighted with lead wire secured on each side of hook shank. Wrap with 3/16'' wide strip of heavy-duty latex dyed dark grey to dark brown.*
THORAX — *Tied in two sections. – Rough looped dubbing of dark brown dyed rabbit fur and guard hairs to form thorax and legs simultaneously. Then tie in wing-case cut to shape from dark brown heavy duty latex. Repeat the thorax, legs and wingcase.*
ANTENNA — *Same as tail*
COMMENT — *Various colors can be obtained by using Pantone or other similar waterproof marker.*

BROWN STONE

HOOK — *Mustad 9672 or 38941 ; sizes 6 to 10*
THREAD — *Brown*
TAIL — *Medium brown goose quill barbules tied in a ''V''*
ABDOMEN — *Medium brown spun fur or wool*
RIB — *Narrow bronze peacock herl alongside fine oval gold tinsel*
THORAX — *Same as abdomen, tied ticker*
WINGCASE — *None*
LEGS — *Grizzly hackle dyed brown, wound over thorax*
COMMENT — *This ''round style'' pattern is favored by some anglers because it presents a uniform silhouette when viewed from any side.*

LITTLE GREEN STONE

HOOK — *Mustad 9672 or 94831 ; sizes 10 to 16*
THREAD — *Yellow*
TAIL — *Light yellowish-green goose quill barbules*
ABDOMEN — *Fluorescent yellow floss, lacquered*
RIB — *Insect green thread*
THORAX — *Light insect green dubbing*
WINGCASE — *Insect green nylon raffia*
LEGS — *Light partridge dyed light yellow olive, tied at throat and spread to each side.*

MONTANA

HOOK — *Mustad 9672 or 38941 ; sizes 2 to 12*
THREAD — *Black*
TAIL — *Black goose quill barbules or hackle barbules*
ABDOMEN — *Black chenille*
THORAX — *Yellow chenille*
LEGS — *Black hackle palmered over thorax*
WINGCASE — *Two strands black chenille tied down over top of thorax*
COMMENT — *A popular, yet simple stonefly pattern, usually weighted.*

YELLOW STONE

HOOK — *Mustad 9672 or 38941 ; sizes 6 to 12*
THREAD — *Yellow*
TAIL — *Ginger goose quill barbules tied in a ''V''*
ABDOMEN — *Weighted. Pale yellow dubbing*
SHELLBACK — *Speckled turkey dyed yellow*
RIB — *Light brown heavy thread*
THORAX — *Same as abdomen*
LEGS — *Grey partridge dyed yellow with stem tied on top of thorax.*
WINGCASE — *Darkly marked speckled turkey, dyed yellow*

HOOK — *Mustad 37160 or similar ; sizes 12 to 18*
THREAD — *Black*
ABDOMEN — *Medium brown synthetic dubbing*
RIB — *Very fine gold tinsel*
WING — *Short section of mallard wing quill tied on each side*
LEGS — *6 to 8 grouse hackle barbules*
THORAX — *Dark brown dubbing, slightly picked out on bottom*
COMMENT — *A basic pupa pattern which can be varied to match natural insect. Other common colors are shades of olive, grey, and brown, all with a dark thorax and head.*

HOOK — *Mustad 37160 or similar ; sizes 12 to 18*
THREAD — *Black*
ABDOMEN — *Bright green synthetic dubbing*
THORAX — *Dark brown dubbing, slightly picked out on bottom*
LEGS — *6 to 8 Grouse hackle barbules*
COMMENT — *This basic caddis larva style can be varied by changing the body color to olive, tan, grey, or cream.*

HOOK — *Mustad 3906 or similar ; sizes 8 to 14*
THREAD — *Grey*
TAIL — *Few grey hackle fibers*
BODY — *Blend of 2/3rd medium grey, 1/3rd light olive synthetic dubbing*
SHELLBACK — *Clear plastic strip cut from heavy duty polybag*
RIB — *Fine silver wire over body and shellback*
LEGS — *Pick out fur on bottom of body*
COMMENT — *Also tied in brown, tan, grey, and olive, to match naturals.*

HOOK — *Mustad 79580 or 9575 or 38941 ; sizes 6 to 10*
THREAD — *Black*
TAIL — *Black goose quill fibers taken from short side of quill*
ABDOMEN — *Black floss*
RIB — *Black ostrich herl over abdomen*
WING CASE — *Black goose quill section pulled over top of completed thorax and legs.*
THORAX — *Dubbed black fur under which is strip of red wool*
LEGS — *Black hackle palmered over thorax, plus at head goose quill fibers tied at each side to flare outward.*

HOOK — *Mustad 79580 ; sizes 8 to 14*
THREAD — *Olive*
TAIL — *Short bunch olive maribou fibers*
ABDOMEN — *Bright green floss ribbed with narrow silver tinsel, overwrapped with flat monofilament.*
WING CASE — *Olive duck wing quill segment*
THORAX — *Dark olive dubbing*
LEGS — *Hen grizzly dyed olive, wound as collar*
EYES — *Cut a pair of connected beads from bead chain, paint black, and tie in at head.*
COMMENT — *When tied in yellow, grey, or brown, will match other damselfly species.*

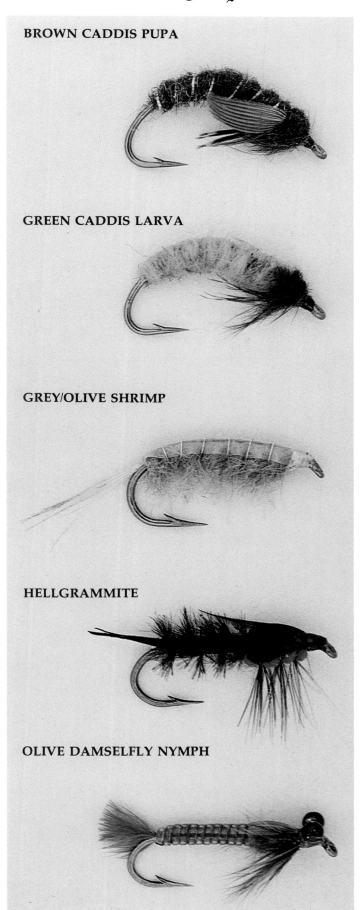

BROWN CADDIS PUPA

GREEN CADDIS LARVA

GREY/OLIVE SHRIMP

HELLGRAMMITE

OLIVE DAMSELFLY NYMPH

35

BLACK NOSE DACE

HOOK — *Mustad 38941 or 9672 ; sizes 6 to 14*
THREAD — *Black*
TAIL — *Short red wool*
BODY — *Flat silver tinsel*
RIB — *Oval silver tinsel*
WING — *White bucktail, over which is black bucktail, over which is brown bucktail.*

DARK EDSON TIGER

HOOK — *Mustad 9575 or 79580 ; sizes 6 to 12*
THREAD — *Yellow*
TAG — *Flat gold tinsel*
TAIL — *Two yellow hackle tips*
BODY — *Yellow chenille – keep a slim shape*
THROAT — *Two red hackle tips*
WING — *Small amount of brown portion of a bucktail dyed yellow*
CHEEK — *Jungle cock (optional)*

LITTLE BROOK TROUT

HOOK — *Mustad 9575 or 79580 ; sizes 4 to 14*
THREAD — *Black*
TAIL — *Red floss over which is small amount of bright green bucktail*
BODY — *Cream spun fur*
RIB — *Flat silver tinsel*
THROAT — *Small bunch orange bucktail*
WING — *Equal bunches: white bucktail, over which is orange bucktail, over which is bright green bucktail. Over this is equal bunch of barred badger (or grey squirrel).*
CHEEK — *Jungle cock (optional)*

LITTLE BROWN TROUT

HOOK — *Mustad 9575 or 79580 ; sizes 4 to 14*
THREAD — *Black*
TAIL — *Small bronze ringneck pheasant breast feather, curved upward*
BODY — *White spun fur*
RIB — *Copper wire or fine gold flat tinsel*
WING — *Equal bunches: yellow bucktail, over which red-orange bucktail, over which dark grey squirrel tail, over which dark red squirrel tail.*
CHEEK — *Jungle cock (optional)*

LITTLE RAINBOW TROUT

HOOK — *Mustad 9575 or 79580 ; sizes 4 to 14*
THREAD — *Black*
TAIL — *Bright green bucktail*
BODY — *Pale pink spun fur*
RIB — *Flat silver tinsel*
THROAT — *Pink bucktail, short*
WING — *Equal bunches: white bucktail, over which pink bucktail, over which bright green bucktail, over which barred badger (or grey squirrel).*
CHEEK — *Jungle cock (optional)*

HOOK — *Mustad 38941 or 9672 ; sizes 6 to 12*
THREAD — *Black*
TAIL — *Soft grizzly barbules*
BODY — *Red floss or wool*
RIB — *Oval gold tinsel*
WING — *Woodchuck body hair using both the marked guard hairs and the light colored soft underfur.*
HACKLE — *Soft grizzly, collared and slightly tied back*
COMMENT — *A recently revived pattern which enjoys growing popularity. A painted white eye with black pupil is optional.*

HOOK — *Mustad 38941 or 9672 ; sizes 4 to 14*
THREAD — *Black*
BODY — *Flat silver tinsel*
RIB — *Oval silver tinsel*
WING — *Small bunch yellow bucktail over which is equal size bunch of red bucktail, over which is a larger bunch of yellow bucktail, equal in size to the first two combined.*
COMMENT — *Probably the best known of all trout flies. It is still a very popular attractor fly.*

HOOK — *Eagle Claw Keel Hook ; sizes 4 to 14*
THREAD — *Black*
TAIL — *None*
BODY — *Flat silver tinsel*
RIB — *Oval silver tinsel*
WING — *White bucktail, over which is equal amount of red bucktail, over which is equal amount of white bucktail.*
COMMENT — *Keel hooks ride upside down making the fly weedless. There are other variations of this pattern.*

HOOK — *Mustad 36620 ; sizes 4 to 12*
THREAD — *Red*
BODY — *Silver embossed tinsel, wrapped on rear 2/3rd of shank*
WING — *Back: Tie in brown bucktail, over which pink/purple bucktail, both extending forward. Stomach: White bucktail, also tied forward. Secure all the way to hook eye, move thread back 1/3rd on shank. Fold bucktail toward rear, keeping colors separated, and tie down, making thin red band of thread. Epoxy head and paint eye.*
COMMENT — *Other bucktails may be tied using this method. A common mistake is using too much bucktail, the fly should be tied sparse.*

HOOK — *Mustad 38941 or 9672 ; sizes 6 to 12*
THREAD — *Black*
TAG — *Flat gold tinsel*
TAIL — *Narrow section of red duck quill*
BODY — *Orange-yellow loose wool or dubbing*
RIB — *Oval gold tinsel*
THROAT — *Yellow hackle collar, tied down.*
WING — *Light brown bucktail*

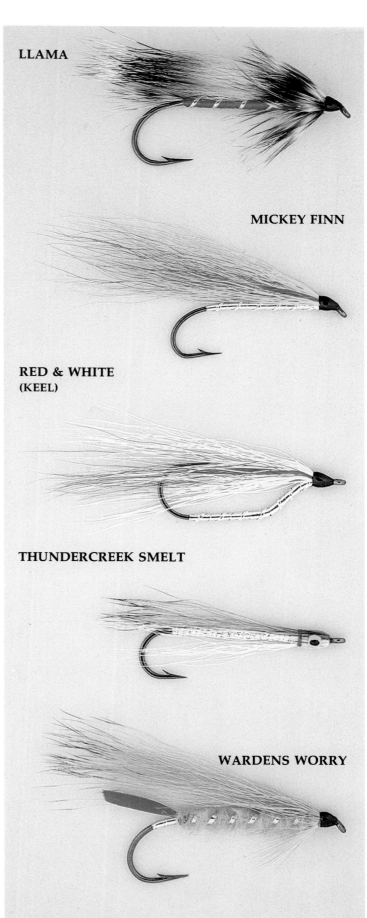

LLAMA

MICKEY FINN

RED & WHITE (KEEL)

THUNDERCREEK SMELT

WARDENS WORRY

37

BADGER MATUKA

HOOK — *Mustad 9672 or 79580 ; sizes 4 to 10*
THREAD — *Black*
BODY — *Cream/yellow synthetic yarn or dubbing with small amount of red dubbing at throat.*
RIB — *Fine oval gold tinsel*
WING — *4 badger hackles tied in at front. Raise and separate hackle fibers on top of body and wind tinsel rib through separations, binding down hackles.*
HACKLE — *Badger hackle collared and slightly tied back*

BLACK GHOST

HOOK — *Mustad 9575 or 79580 ; sizes 2 to 12*
THREAD — *Black*
TAIL — *Yellow hackle barbules*
BODY — *Black floss or black wool*
RIB — *Flat silver tinsel*
WING — *White saddle hackle*
THROAT — *Yellow hackle barbules, beard style*
CHEEK — *Jungle cock*

CARDINELLE

HOOK — *Mustad 9575 or 79580 ; sizes 2 to 10*
THREAD — *Fluorescent red or orange*
BODY — *Fluorescent red or orange wool*
UNDERWING — *Fluorescent red synthetic hair*
OVERWING — *Cerise maribou*
HACKLE — *Longish yellow saddle hackle, collared and tied back.*

COLONEL BATES

HOOK — *Mustad 9575 or 9672 ; sizes 2 to 12*
THREAD — *Red*
TAIL — *Small section red duck wing quill*
BODY — *Flat silver tinsel*
WING — *Two yellow saddle hackles with a slightly shorter white saddle hackle on each side.*
THROAT — *Small bunch dark brown hackle barbules, beard style*
SHOULDER — *Teal breast feather over 1/3 length of wing*

DARK HORNBERG

HOOK — *Mustad 9671 or similar ; sizes 6 to 16*
THREAD — *Brown*
BODY — *Dubbing mixture of 1/3 tan, 1/3 olive, and 1/3 muskrat.*
WING — *Bronze mallard flank tied tent shape on top. It helps to fold outside edges of feather under stem before tying down.*
HACKLE — *Mixed brown and dark blue dun*
COMMENT — *The Hornberg style has been so successful that many other variations exist, with cinnamon, yellow, and pale blue wings with matching hackles being the most common.*

38

HOOK — *Mustad 9672 or 38941 ; sizes 4 to 10*
THREAD — *Black*
TAIL — *Four peacock sword strands*
BODY — *Rear 1/3 red floss, front 2/3 peacock herl*
WING — *Two furnace hackles*
HACKLE — *Furnace hackle collared and slightly tied back.*
COMMENT — *Sometimes grizzly hackle dyed brown is substituted for Furnace. Frequently tied with wing splayed to each side.*

HOOK — *Mustad 9672 or 79580 ; sizes 3/0 to 6*
THREAD — *White*
BODY — *Wrap entire hook shank with thread, coat with cement, then tie on hollow primary quill of turkey or goose which has end filled with cork painted white.*
WING — *Olive maribou tied in above cork and tied down by wrapping thread in wide turns to bend and back forward.*
EYE — *Yellow with black pupil*
MARKINGS — *Red dots painted on body*

HOOK — *Mustad 9575 or 79580 ; sizes 6 to 10*
THREAD — *Black*
TAIL — *Golden pheasant crest*
BODY — *Yellow floss*
RIB — *Flat gold tinsel*
WING — *Bronze mallard flank*
HACKLE — *Bright orange hackle collared and tied back*

HOOK — *Mustad 9575 or 9672 ; sizes 2 to 12*
THREAD — *Black*
BODY — *Golden yellow floss*
RIB — *Flat silver tinsel*
THROAT — *4 or 5 peacock herl strands next to body, then sparse white bucktail, then short golden pheasant crest.*
WING — *Underwing ; golden pheasant crest full length of body. Overwing ; 4 grey saddle hackle.*
SHOULDER — *Silver pheasant body feather, 1/3 wing length*
CHEEK — *Jungle cock*
COMMENT — *Original patterns show variation in wing color from pale olive/grey to medium blue dun. This is New England's best known streamer pattern.*

HOOK — *Mustad 9671 or similar ; sizes 6 to 16*
THREAD — *Black*
BODY — *Flat silver tinsel*
WING — *Underwing ; sparse yellow hackle barbules. Overwing ; mallard flank folded and applied tent shape over body.*
HACKLE — *Brown and grizzly mixed*
COMMENT — *The original Hornberg was tied with mallard flanks, one on each side, with jungle cock eyes. Often the mallard flank tips were cemented. The above version seems more effective. Smaller sizes are frequently fished as dry flies.*

DARK SPRUCE

FLOATING QUILL MINNOW

GOLDEN DEMON

GREY GHOST

HORNBERG

39

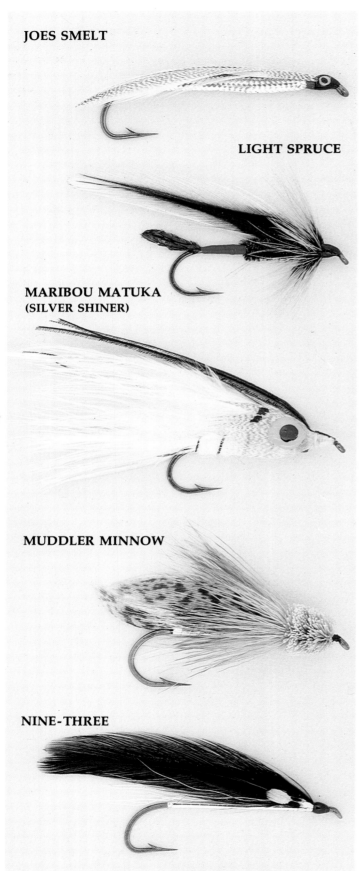

JOES SMELT

LIGHT SPRUCE

**MARIBOU MATUKA
(SILVER SHINER)**

MUDDLER MINNOW

NINE-THREE

HOOK — *Mustad 9575 or 79580 ; sizes 2 to 6*
THREAD — *Red*
TAIL — *Short red hackle barbules*
BODY — *Braided mylar tinsel with cotton core removed. Hook shank is inserted through tinsel which is then tied at rear and front with red thread and cemented.*
WING — *Pintail flank or long mallard flank tied flat over top*
HEAD — *Black with painted yellow eye and black pupil*

HOOK — *Mustad 9672 or 38941 ; sizes 4 to 10*
THREAD — *Black*
TAIL — *4 peacock sword fibers*
BODY — *Rear 1/3 red floss, front 2/3 peacock herl*
WING — *Two light badger hackles*
COLLAR — *Light badger hackle collared and tied back*
COMMENT — *Also tied as a wet fly for Cutthroat trout. Frequently tied with wing splayed to each side.*

HOOK — *Mustad 38941 or similar ; sizes 2 to 8*
THREAD — *White*
TAIL — *2 fine silver mylar strands extending to end of wing*
BODY — *White sparkle yarn tied heavy with a small band of red wool at throat.*
RIB — *Heavy black thread*
WING — *2 maribou feathers extending to end of tail, one bound down against body matuka style, the second on top.*
CHEEK — *Mallard breast feathers, each coated with lacquer or vinyl cement around eye area and painted with yellow eye and black pupil.*
TOPPING — *2 strands fine silver mylar over which 3 strands peacock herl.*

HOOK — *Mustad 9672 or 38941 ; sizes 1/0 to 14*
THREAD — *Brown*
TAIL — *Section from mottled turkey quill*
BODY — *Gold tinsel wrapped over rear 2/3 of hook shank*
WING — *Underwing of grey squirrel (some use brown calftail), overwing of paired sections of speckled turkey quill, tied on edge.*
HEAD — *Spun grey/brown deer body hair, front part clipped to shape, leaving a collar of hair at rear of head.*
COMMENT — *Fished wet or dry, weighted or unweighted, and in various colors (yellow, white, black and green) this is one of the best flies around.*

HOOK — *Mustad 9575 or 9672 ; sizes 2 to 12*
THREAD — *Black*
BODY — *Flat silver tinsel*
WING — *Underwing ; a small bunch of white bucktail. Overwing ; 2 green saddle hackles flanked by 2 black saddle hackles.*
CHEEKS — *Jungle cock*
COMMENT — *Originally, the fly had green saddle tied flat over shank and black saddle tied on edge above.*

OLIVE MATUKA

HOOK — *Mustad 9672 or 79580 ; sizes 4 to 10*
THREAD — *Olive*
BODY — *Olive synthetic yarn or dubbing with small amount of red dubbing at throat.*
RIB — *Fine oval silver tinsel*
WING — *4 grizzly hackles dyed dark olive, secured down by rib as with Badger Matuka.*
HACKLE — *Grizzly hackle dyed olive collared and slightly tied back.*

SPUDDLER

HOOK — *Mustad 79580 or 9672 ; sizes 2 to 10*
THREAD — *Brown*
TAIL — *Short bunch brown calftail*
BODY — *Rear 3/4 cream dubbed fur, next 1/4 red fur. Total body is 3/4 of hook shank.*
WING — *Tie in small bunch brown calftail, extending body length. Then, tie in 4 grizzly hackles, dyed brown. Add a small bunch of short red squirrel on each side of wing.*
COLLAR — *Brown antelope hair spun on with tips toward rear*
HEAD — *Brown antelope hair spun on and clipped short top and bottom. Sides clipped to overall bullet shape as viewed from top.*

SUPERVISOR

HOOK — *Mustad 9575 or 9672 ; sizes 2 to 12*
THREAD — *Black*
TAIL — *Short thin red wool*
BODY — *Flat silver tinsel*
RIB — *Oval silver tinsel*
WING — *Underwing ; sparse bunch of white bucktail. Overwing ; 4 light blue saddle hackles.*
SHOULDER — *Pale green hackles, 2/3rd length of wing, one on each side.*
CHEEKS — *Jungle cock*
TOPPING — *4 or 5 strands of peacock herl*

WHITE MARIBOU MUDDLER

HOOK — *Mustad 9672 or 38941 ; sizes 2 to 12*
THREAD — *White*
TAIL — *Red hackle barbules*
BODY — *Silver tinsel chenille*
WING — *Underwing ; small bunch grey or red squirrel over which is longer white maribou. Top with 4 or 5 strands of peacock herl.*
HEAD — *Grey/brown deer body hair tied same as on Muddler Minnow.*
COMMENT — *Often weighted, also popular in black, grey, brown, olive, & yellow.*

WHITLOCK SCULPIN

HOOK — *Mustad 7970 or 9672 ; sizes 1/0 to 8*
THREAD — *Tan*
BODY — *Weighted. Cream dubbed fur with red dubbed throat.*
RIB — *Oval gold tinsel*
WING — *2 or 3 variegated cree neck hackles tied flat over which a shorter wide brown partridge or grouse feather. Above and on each side are shorter bunches of red squirrel.*
CHEEKS — *On each side a breast feather, curved outward, from hen pheasant or hen mallard duck.*
COLLAR — *Red/brown deer body hair on top so tips point toward rear ; caribou below.*
HEAD — *In bands, first dark brown on top with grey deer body below ; second all brown deer body hair.*
COMMENT — *Colors may vary to match natural sculpins.*

41

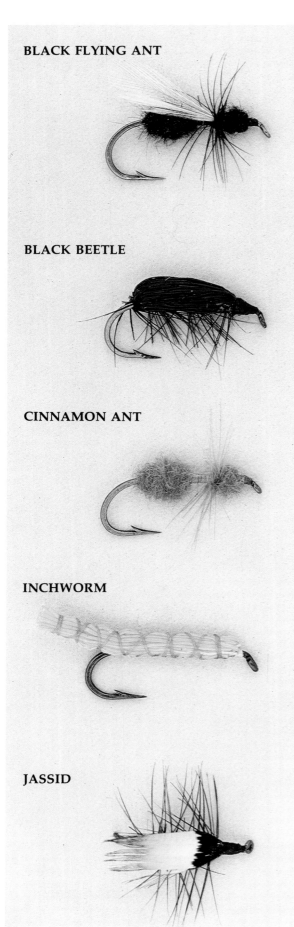

BLACK FLYING ANT

HOOK — *Mustad 94840 or similar ; sizes 10 to 20*
THREAD — *Black*
BODY — *Tie in two distinct segments using black dubbed fur. The abdomen is slightly larger than the head.*
LEGS — *Before tying head, wrap 1 or 2 turns of black hackle rear of head.*
WINGS — *Before tying head apply 2 light blue dun hackle points splayed one to each side, down wing style.*
COMMENT — *Can also be tied without wings or as a wet fly using lacquered black floss for the body.*

BLACK BEETLE

HOOK — *Mustad 94840 or similar ; sizes 10 to 18*
THREAD — *Black*
BODY — *Lay foundation of thread, coat with vinyl cement, tie in the butt ends of a fat bunch of dyed black deer body hair with tips extending well past rear of hook.*
LEGS — *Black hackle palmered over body*
SHELLBACK — *Fold deer hair over top of body, tie down, clip excess, and form head. Clip hackle on bottom and coat shellback with vinyl cement.*

CINNAMON ANT

HOOK — *Mustad 94840 or similar ; sizes 12 to 22*
THREAD — *Orange*
BODY — *Tied in two distinct segments using an orangish-brown dubbing. The abdomen is slightly larger than the head. Leave a space between segments, wrapped thinly with tying thread.*
LEGS — *One or two turns of ginger hackle wrapped immediately behind head.*
COMMENT — *Can also be tied with light blue dun wings as on the Black Flying Ant.*

INCHWORM

HOOK — *Mustad 94831 or similar ; sizes 12 and 14*
THREAD — *Insect green*
BODY — *Wrap hook shank with tying thread, leaving thread at rear. Take long bunch (20-24 strands) of deer body hair dyed insect green and lay parallel to top of hook so middle of bunch is above hook eye. Wrap thread forward in well-spaced turns. Fold back the deer hair, thus making a double bunch, and loosely wrap full length, even beyond hook bend, and return thread to head and tie off. Finished fly should be coated with vinyl cement.*

JASSID

HOOK — *Mustad 94840 or similar ; sizes 14 to 22*
THREAD — *Black*
BODY — *A black hackle palmered length of shank, then clipped short on top and bottom.*
WING — *A single jungle cock eye tied flat on top of body*
COMMENT — *This simple pattern has proved successful on difficult trout. It imitates various beetles and leafhoppers. Different colored hackles are sometimes used.*

JOES HOPPER

LETORT CRICKET

LETORT HOPPER

CRAYFISH

LEECH

HOOK — *Mustad 9672 or 94831 ; sizes 6 to 12*
THREAD — *Brown*
TAIL — *Red hackle barbules*
BODY — *Light yellow acrylic wool or polypropylene. Extend body by first placing loop of wool over tail, then wind body.*
RIB — *Brown hackle. After wrapping, trim hackle to slight taper, longest at rear.*
WING — *Speckled turkey wing quill sections tied at each side with tips curving upward.*
HACKLE — *Mixed brown and grizzly*

HOOK — *Mustad 9671 or 94831 ; sizes 8 to 14*
THREAD — *Black*
BODY — *Dubbed black rabbit*
WING — *Section from black goose quill tied flat over body*
OVERWING — *Tie on top a clump of black deer body hair, the tips extending rearward past bend of hook.*
HEAD — *Short section of spun black deer body hair clipped fairly short*

HOOK — *Mustad 9671 or 94831 ; sizes 8 to 14*
THREAD — *Yellow*
BODY — *Yellow dubbing*
WING — *Section of speckled turkey quill tied flat over body*
OVERWING — *Tie on top a clump of natural grey/brown deer body hair, the tips extending rearward past bend of hook.*
HEAD — *Short section of spun natural deer body hair clipped fairly short*
COMMENT — *Also tied with body colors of tan, green, orange, or a blend of colors.*

HOOK — *Mustad 3906B or similar ; sizes 4 to 10*
THREAD — *Brown*
TAIL (Actually claws) — *Two bunches of light color red squirrel tail splayed to each side.*
BODY — *Olive green wool*
RIB — *Brown hackle palmered over body*
SHELLBACK — *Section from brown goose quill, well lacquered once fly is completed.*
COMMENT — *Coloration may vary depending on geography and time of year. Fly is tied in reverse to imitate the backward swimming motion of the crayfish.*

HOOK — *Mustad 9672 or 38941 ; sizes 4 to 10*
THREAD — *Claret*
TAIL — *Thick clump of claret maribou, clip to 2/3rds of body length.*
BODY — *Claret mohair or similar, tied to be thick at rear, tapering forward*
HACKLE — *Very sparse soft claret hackle collared*
COMMENT — *Before tying, bend hook as shown and weight rear portion. Also tied in black, olive, and various shades of brown.*

Steelhead Flies

BLACK BEAR

HOOK — *Mustad 36890 or Eagle Claw 1197 ; sizes 1 to 6*
THREAD — *Black*
TAIL — *Black and red hackle, mixed*
BODY — *Black chenille*
RIB — *Oval silver tinsel*
HACKLE — *Black and red hackle, mixed*
WING — *Black bucktail*

BRADS BRAT

HOOK — *Mustad 36890 or Eagle Claw 1197 ; sizes 4 to 8*
THREAD — *White*
TIP — *Flat gold tinsel*
TAIL — *Orange bucktail over which is white bucktail.*
BODY — *Rear 1/2 orange wool, front 1/2 red wool*
RIB — *Flat gold tinsel*
HACKLE — *Dark brown hackle collared, tied down*
WING — *White bucktail, over which is orange bucktail, white dominating.*

FALL FAVORITE

HOOK — *Mustad 36890 or Eagle Claw 1197 ; sizes 1 to 6*
THREAD — *Red*
BODY — *Embossed silver tinsel wrapped over an underbody of white floss, tapered.*
HACKLE — *Scarlet, collared and tied down*
WING — *Hot orange calf tail or bucktail*

GOLD COMET

HOOK — *Mustad 36890 or Eagle Claw 1197 ; sizes 2 to 6*
THREAD — *Orange*
TAIL — *Orange calf tail*
BODY — *Oval gold tinsel wrapped over an underbody of yellow floss, slightly tapered.*
HACKLE — *Yellow and hot orange collar tied back.*
EYES — *Brass bead chain*
COMMENT — *Also known as Coles Comet. This and Silver Comet are the most popular of the series.*

ORANGE OPTIC

HOOK — *Mustad 7970 ; size 2*
THREAD — *Black*
BODY — *Oval silver tinsel*
HACKLE — *Scarlet, beard style*
WING — *Orange bucktail*
HEAD — *Split bead painted black with white eye and red pupil.*
COMMENT — *One of several in the ''optic'' series. A favorite that sinks very well.*

44

HOOK — *Mustad 36890 or Eagle Claw 1197, sizes 1 to 8*
THREAD — *Black*
TAIL — *Golden Pheasant tippets*
BODY — *Rear and front 1/4 are peacock herl, middle half scarlet floss.*
HACKLE — *Coachman brown collar tied down*
WING — *White bucktail*

ROYAL COACHMAN

HOOK — *Mustad 36890 or Eagle Claw 1197 ; sizes 1 to 8*
THREAD — *Black*
TAIL — *Mallard flank tied short*
BODY — *Black chenille*
RIB — *Oval silver tinsel*
HACKLE — *Grizzly collar tied back*
WING — *Grizzly hackle tips splayed away from each other and extending to end of tail.*

SILVER HILTON

HOOK — *Mustad 36890 or Eagle Claw 1197 ; sizes 1 to 6*
THREAD — *Black*
TAIL — *Scarlet hackle barbules*
BODY — *Black chenille*
RIB — *Oval silver tinsel*
HACKLE — *Black collar tied back*
WING — *Black skunk tail over which is a small amount of white skunk tail.*
COMMENT — *Perhaps the best known of the dark steelhead flies.*

SKUNK

45

HOOK — *Mustad 36890 or Eagle Claw 1197 ; sizes 1 to 8*
THREAD — *Black*
TAIL — *Orange hackle barbules*
BODY — *Red chenille*
HACKLE — *Reddish brown collar, tied down*
WING — *White calf tail or bucktail*

THOR

HOOK — *Mustad 36890 or Eagle Claw 1197 ; sizes 1/0 to 6*
THREAD — *Red*
TAIL — *Mixed bunch of scarlet and yellow hackle barbules*
BODY — *Red chenille*
RIB — *Flat silver tinsel*
HACKLE — *Mixed scarlet and yellow, collared and tied down*
WING — *White calf tail or bucktail*

SKYKOMISH

Atlantic Salmon Flies

BLACK BEAR-GREEN BUTT

HOOK — *Mustad 36890 or similar ; sizes 6 to 12*
THREAD — *Black*
TAG — *Oval silver tinsel*
TIP — *Fluorescent green wool of floss*
TAIL — *Golden pheasant crest*
BODY — *Black floss or wool*
RIB — *Oval silver tinsel*
THROAT — *Black hackle collared and tied down*
WING — *Black bear hair or black squirrel tail*

BUTTERFLY

HOOK — *Mustad 7958 ; sizes 4 to 10*
THREAD — *Black*
TAIL — *Bright red hackle fibers*
BUTT — *Fluorescent green wool (This is the most popular addition to the original pattern)*
BODY — *Peacock herl*
WING — *White goat hair or other stiff white hair tied at 45° angle to hook shank and fully splayed.*
HACKLE — *Brown, wrapped once behind wing, then once in front of wing.*

BLUE CHARM

HOOK — *Mustad 36890 or similar ; sizes 2 to 12*
THREAD — *Black*
TAG — *Oval silver tinsel*
TIP — *Golden yellow floss*
BUTT — *Black ostrich herl (optional)*
BODY — *Black floss*
RIB — *Oval silver tinsel*
THROAT — *Teal blue hackle collared and tied down*
WING — *Brown mottled turkey tail with narrow teal flank strips over upper half of wing.*
TOPPING — *Golden pheasant crest*

COBURN SPECIAL

HOOK — *Mustad 36890 or similar ; sizes 1/0 to 6*
THREAD — *Black or fluorescent green*
TAG — *Oval silver tinsel*
TAIL — *Monga ringtail, dyed green, over which a small portion of black monga ringtail.*
BODY — *Fluorescent green floss built up to cigar shape with several turns of black ostrich herl in the middle.*
WING — *Same as tail*
THROAT — *Yellow hackle collared and tied back*
COMMENT — *A new pattern which has proved to be outstanding at the Bangor Salmon Pool.*

COSSEBOOM

HOOK — *Mustad 36890 or similar ; sizes 1/0 to 10*
THREAD — *Red*
TAG — *Embossed silver tinsel*
TAIL — *Light olive floss*
BODY — *Light olive floss*
RIB — *Embossed silver tinsel*
WING — *Grey squirrel*
CHEEK — *Jungle cock (usually omitted)*
HACKLE — *Lemon yellow hackle, collared and tied back*

HOOK — *Mustad 36890 or similar ; sizes 2 to 10*
THREAD — *Black*
TAG — *Flat silver tinsel*
TIP — *Pale yellow floss*
TAIL — *Golden pheasant crest*
BUTT — *Black ostrich herl*
BODY — *Rear 1/3 yellow floss, front 2/3 bright grass-green seal or substitute*
RIB — *Oval silver tinsel over entire body ; also bright grass-green hackle palmered over front 2/3 body.*
WING — *Underwing of strands of golden pheasant tippet over which sparse mixed yellow and green bucktail over which sparse brown bucktail.*
HACKLE — *Bright yellow, collared and tied down*

HOOK — *Mustad 36890 or similar ; sizes 4 to 10*
THREAD — *Fluorescent red*
TAG — *Flat gold tinsel*
TIP — *Yellow floss*
TAIL — *Golden pheasant crest*
BODY — *Black floss*
RIB — *Oval gold tinsel*
WING — *Black squirrel tail*
THROAT — *Fluorescent orange hackle, beard style*
COMMENT — *The hot orange has proved to be a fly which produced when all others failed, particularly in Labrador.*

HOOK — *Mustad 36890 or similar ; sizes 4 to 10*
THREAD — *Black*
TAG — *Oval silver tinsel*
TIP — *Golden yellow floss*
TAIL — *Golden pheasant crest over which shorter bunch of scarlet hackle barbules*
BUTT — *Black ostrich herl*
BODY — *Embossed silver tinsel*
RIB — *Bright yellow hackle tied in by tip and wound forward*
WING — *Light brown bucktail*
HACKLE — *Bright orange hackle, collared and tied back*

HOOK — *36890 or similar ; sizes 4 to 10*
THREAD — *Black*
TAG — *Oval silver tinsel*
TIP — *Bright yellow floss*
TAIL — *Three or four peacock sword fibers*
BODY — *Bright kelly green wool or seal fur*
RIB — *Oval silver tinsel*
THROAT — *Bright yellow hackle barbules, beard style, covered by bright green hackle barbules, beard style.*
WING — *Grey fox guard hairs*
CHEEK — *Jungle cock (optional)*

HOOK — *Mustad 36890 or similar ; sizes 4 to 10*
THREAD — *Red*
TAG — *Oval gold tinsel*
TAIL — *3 to 4 peacock sword fibers*
BODY — *Rear 1/2 yellow floss ; front 1/2 peacock herl*
VEILING — *A piece of yellow floss tied in before the peacock herl and extending rearward to end of body*
RIB — *Oval gold tinsel*
WING — *Grey fox guard hairs*
CHEEK — *Jungle cock (optional)*
HACKLE — *Grizzly hackle collared and tied back*

GREEN HIGHLANDER

HOT ORANGE

ORANGE BLOSSOM

47

ROGERS FANCY

RUSTY RAT

Index of Fly Patterns